ORIGINAL PATENTEES OF LAND
at
WASHINGTON
Prior to 1700

I0029924

By
Bessie Wilmarth Gahn

CLEARFIELD

Originally published
Washington, 1936

Reprinted by
Genealogical Publishing Company
Baltimore, Maryland,
1969

Library of Congress Catalogue Card Number 77-77982

Reprinted for Clearfield Company by
Genealogical Publishing Company
Baltimore, Maryland
1998, 2011

ISBN 978-0-8063-1900-1

Made in the United States of America

ORIGINAL PATENTEES *of* LAND *at* WASHINGTON
PRIOR TO 1700

Dedicated

To my Great (7th)-Grandfather

COLONEL GERARD FOWKE

Who represented Westmoreland County, Virginia, in the
Council at Jamestown, and later
Represented Charles County, Maryland,
In the Assembly at St. Marys

by

BESSIE WILMARTH GAHN

1936

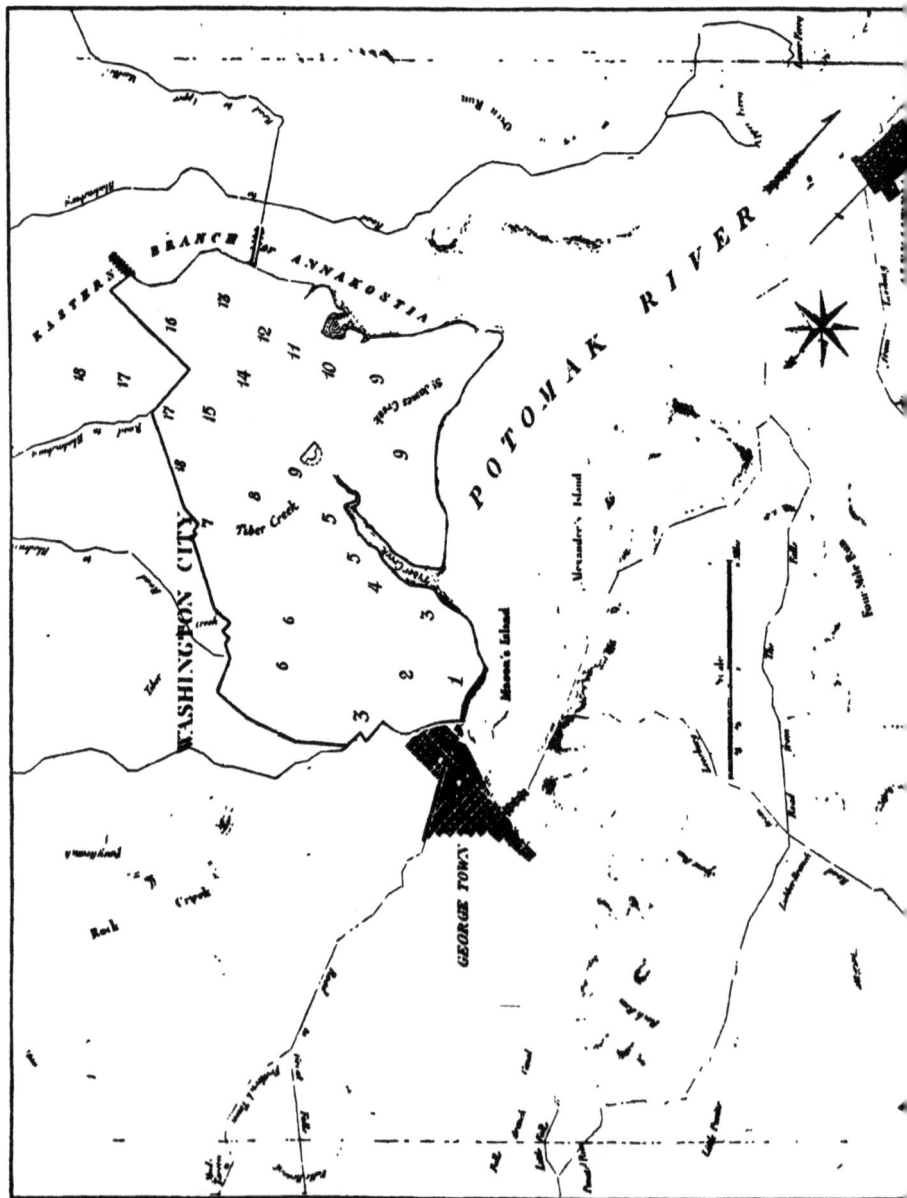

ORIGINAL PATENTEES
OF
LAND AT WASHINGTON

1. William Hutchison
2. John Watson
3. John Langworth
4. John Lewger
5. Richard and
   William Pinner
6. John Peerce
7. Francis Pope
8. Robert Troope
9. George Thompson
10. Walter Houp
11. Walter Thompson
12. Andrew Clarke
13. Zachariah Wade
14. Richard Evans
15. William Atcheson
16. Walter Evans
17. Henry Jowles
18. Ninian Beall

FOREWORD

In reading the court records of the Seventeenth Century one finds spelling that is unsettled and capricious. A common English word will be spelled in several different ways by the same writer, even on the same page. For instance, Hutchison, Hutchinson, Hutchins, and Hutchings.

In addition to unsettled spelling, the searcher of early records encounters inconsistency in geographic names. One can sympathize with this difficulty by placing himself in the Royal Office at London at that period or at the tiny settlement at Saint Marys, and, unfamiliar with the terrain of the New World, try to designate the location of an estate in the far regions where few, if any, of the places have received names. Indian names, many of them unknown to European languages, will be repeated according to the apprehension of their meaning in the vernacular of the colonist. Thus, the creeks, rivers, islands, in the vicinity of the Nacotchtank Indians, who inhabited both shores of the Potomac River.

In the preparation of this book on the first patentees, before 1700, of land in the original District of Columbia, accounts have been taken, frequently verbatim, from the Archives of Maryland and the Henning Statues of Virginia. In addition, records have been used from the courthouse at La Plata, for Charles County, Md.; at Upper Marlboro, for Prince Georges County Md.; at Annapolis, for the Province of Maryland; at Manassas, for Prince William County, Va.; at the Virginia Land Office in Richmond; at Rockville, for Montgomery County, Md.; at Frederick, Md., for records in that county; at the Office of Recorder of Deeds, District of Columbia, and in the files of the Supreme Court, District of Columbia. Excellent guidance has been obtained from such historical books as those of Neill, J. Winsor, J. T. Scharf, Fairfax Harrison, Chas. W. Stetson, Allen C. Clark, W. B. Bryan, and many others, especially the Early Settlers' Lists in the Rare Book Room of the Library of Congress.

Bessie Wilmarth Gahn

April 1, 1936
Washington, D. C.

PART ONE

The Shorelines

TO arrive off the waterfront of the Nation's Capital in the sunshine of early morning, after a restful night up the Potomac, is an exceedingly pleasant experience. The shore lines leading to Washington are graced with welcoming trees and river banks still green with native flora. Wild birds of various kinds pour forth their morning melodies, and here and there the wild duck and the long-legged heron watch near the shores for a school of early-morning fish. Sunlight sparkles on the water and flashes on shore where an early car skims along the drives.

Straight ahead of our ship the river breaks into three branches. There is the western, or main Potomac, with its four splendid bridges; then the central, or narrow ship-channel between Hains Point and the Army War College; lastly, the Eastern Branch, or Anacostia River, bordered on the west by the Navy Yard, and on the east by the Naval Airport. The two peninsulas thus formed, Hains Point, gay in spring with cherry blossoms and visitors, and the grounds of the stately War College, are first to greet ships up the Potomac. Not far inland, the white-pointed shaft of the Washington Monument glistens against the sky, and to the east across the city the staunch white dome of the Nation's Capitol lends historic dignity. The picture truly is alluring, but to history lovers who can vision the scene 300 years ago, this early-morning arrival brings a thrill. Suppose, for instance, we turn back to the year 1636. What differences shall we find?

First, Hains Point, like the lost Atlantis, will disappear with its teahouse and visitors and cherry trees, leaving a broad stretch of water from the War College peninsula, to Virginia. On the War College peninsula the buildings and statue and fine lawns will turn into broad fields leading out toward Turkey Buzzard Point, so named on the map of Augus-

tine Herman of 1673 and on subsequent early maps of Robert
Brooke and of John F. A. Priggs.

To the right, the Anacostia River broadens into a wide
bay devoid of Navy Yard or ships. The Naval Airport to the
east melts away and even the very ground on which it stands,
leaving wide stretches of wild rice along the shore. On the
gentle sloping banks threads of smoke rise peacefully from
the camp fires of Nacotchtank, the village of the Anacostine
Indians.[1]

Even the ship we are riding must change. The deck chairs,
the salon, and the passengers disappear. The pilothouse and
smokestacks melt into tall masts and billowing white sails.
Our Star-Spangled Banner disappears, and the Royal Flag of
Great Britain flutters in its stead. Thus, on we sail northward, past untouched, fertile fields, until soon we find another
wide bay on our right. In days of old this wide bay was the
mouth of Tiber Creek. Subsequently it was called Goose
Creek, and then reverted to Tiber. Today (1936) the water of
this creek has disappeared, and the area is covered by land-
scaped terraces and elegant drives surrounding the Lincoln
Memorial. In 1636, as today, we sail past a handsome wooded
island on the west, and around its northern end we turn with
the river, so that our course is due west instead of north. No
sooner have we turned than we pass the wide mouth of Rock
Creek with its steep, rocky hillsides of long ago. Up on these
tree-covered heights (now Georgetown) we see again those
peaceful curls of rising smoke announcing human life and
camp fires, and we know we have reached Tohoga, the site
whose charms were sung by Henry Fleet in his Journals of
1632.

––––––

Henry Fleet, the First Promoter

Henry Fleet was one of the seven sons of William and
Deborah Fleet of Chartham, Kent (Genesis of the United
States, Brown, vol. 2, p. 892). With three of his brothers, Edward, Reynold, and John, he came to Virginia in 1623, but
soon after arrival, on a trading expedition up the Potomac, he

––––––

[1] A map by Graffenreid, 1712, shows the Indian village between the Eastern Branch and the Tiber Creek.

was captured by Indians. Remaining a captive for five years, he became familiar with the Indian tongue. In 1634, as an interpreter and guide, he arrived in Maryland with the colonists and directed them to St. Marys for settlement. Here he received a patent for 2,000 acres of land. In 1638 he and his brothers were members of the Maryland Legislature. Eventually, he returned to Virginia and settled at Fleet's Bay in Lancaster County, where in 1652 he represented the county in the House of Burgesses. His daughter Sarah married Edwin Conway of that county.

Neill, in his "Founders of Maryland," gives the following:

"In the fall of 1621 the ship Warwick and the pinnace Tiger sailed from the Thames with supplies and 38 young women, selected with care as wives for Virginia planters. They arrived at Jamestown. The Tiger was then sent under Spilman, the experienced trader, with 26 men to trade for corn in the upper Potomac. * * * Spilman landed among the Anacostans, who lived on and near the site of the (present) city of Washington. Five men who remained on board were attacked by savages. whom they repulsed by the discharge of cannon. Those on shore were either killed or made prisoners, and among the latter was Henry Fleet. * * * After a captivity of several years, he returned to England."

Fleet's manuscript of the voyage, in journals which he kept, is preserved in the library of the Archbishop of Canterbury, at Lambeth. It was first presented to the American public by Neill in his "English Colonization of America." It is entitled "Brief Journal of a Voyage made in the Bark Virginia to Virginia and Other Parts of the Continent of America." Fleet tells of his voyage first to the coast of New England, and then of his expedition up the Potomac. By his rosy representations, he induced London merchants to engage in the Potomac beaver trade, and in 1631 he returned to America. He writes:

"The fourth of July, 1631, we weighed anchor from the Downs and sailed for New England, where we arrived in the harbor of Pascattouaie the 9th of September, making some study upon the coast of New England. From thence on Monday the 19th of September we sailed directly for Virginia, where we

came to anchor in the bay there the 21st of October.
* * * On Tuesday the 10th of January we set sail
from Point Comfort and arrived at Pascattoway in
New England on Tuesday the 7th of February, where
we delivered our corn, the quantity being 700 bushels.
* * * On Monday the 9th of April, 1632, we weighed
anchor and shaped our course for Virginia. * * * Wed-
nesday the 16th of May, we shaped our course for
the river of Patomack. Monday the 21st of May we
came to anchor at the mouth of the river, where
hastening on shore I sent two Indians in company
with my brother Edward to the Emperor, being three
days' journey towards the Falls. The Nacostines before here (in 1621) occasioned the killing of 20 men
of our English, myself then being taken prisoner
and detained five years, which was in the time of
Sir Francis Wyatt, he being the Governor of Virginia. * * * They (the Indians) came in their birchen
canoes to seek to withdraw me from having any com-
merce with the other Indians, and the Nacostines
were earnest in this matter.

"On Monday the 25th of June we set sail for the
town of Tohoga, when we came to an anchor two
leagues short of the Falls, being in the latitude
of 41, on the 26th of June.

[The First Desccription of Land at Washington]

"This place without all question is the most
pleasant and healthful place in all this country, and
most convenient for habitation, the air temperate in
summer and not violent in winter. It aboundeth with
all manner of fish. The Indians in one night commonly
will catch 30 sturgeon in a place where the river is
not above 12 fathom broad; and as for deer, buf-
faloes, bears, turkeys, the woods do swarm with them,
and the soil is exceedingly fertile; but above this
place the country is rocky and mountainous like
Cannida.

"The 27th of June I manned my shallop and went
up with the flood, the tide rising about four feet in
heigh at this place. We had not rowed above three
miles but we might hear the F'alls to roar about six
miles distant, but which it appears that the river
is separated with rocks, but only in that one place,
for beyond is a fair river."

Immediately after the publication of Fleet's Journals,
across the Atlantic, Englishmen of note became interested,

and ships with colonists soon left England for the new Province granted Lord Baltimore. Father Andrew White, a Jesuit missionary who arrived with the Ark and the Dove in 1634, says of Henry Fleet, in his diary, "The Governor had taken with him as a companion on his voyage, Henry Fleet, a Captain from the Virginia colony, a man especially acceptable to the savages, well versed in their language and acquainted with the country. * * * ("Narrative of a Journey in Maryland" by Father Andrew White.")

Land Allotment in Maryland

In 1636, Lord Baltimore stipulated the terms for allotment of land under his official seal. Every adventurer in the first expedition, 1634, who had transported five men between 15 and 50 years of age, was to receive 2,000 acres of land for a yearly rental of 400 pounds of good wheat. An individual who did not transport five men was to receive 100 acres for himself, a like area for his wife (if he had one), and for each servant, and 50 acres for every child under the age of sixteen. For this he was to pay a yearly rental of 10 pounds of wheat for every 50 acres.

Those who should arrive after 1635 were promised 1,000 acres for every five men they transported to the colony, and the rent for it was fixed at 20 shillings a year, payable in the country's produce. The individual grants of 100 acres for each adult and 50 acres for each child remained the same, the rent being placed at 12 pence for every 50 acres. The tracts were granted to these persons and to their heirs forever. If the owner died without heirs, his land became "escheat" and reverted back to the Lord Proprietary.

Ships from the Old World continued to arrive with settlers for the manors and plantations of lower Maryland. In 1663 began the patents in the upper reaches of the Potomac and near the Falls, the vicinity of which Henry Fleet painted so rosy a picture. Before 1700, the whole area now covered by Washington was in the possession of its first land owners.

New Scotland Hundred

The area in Maryland now included in the District of Columbia, in those days before 1700, was called New Scotland

Hundred, and was a part of Charles County. This county was created by Lord Baltimore in 1658. It was the property along the Potomac River from Wicomico "as high as the settlements extend." In 1695 Mattawoman Creek was made the upper boundary of Charles County, and the territory above it along the river was made into the new county of Prince Georges. The Court then divided the counties into "Hundreds," the region extending from Oxon Branch (opposite Alexandria, Va.) to the falls of the Potomac, receiving the name "New Scotland Hundred," with Daniel Ebbett constable; Charles Beall, pressmaster, and Francis Prisley, overseer of highways. Frederick County was created in 1748 from the upper part of Prince Georges County, beginning at Rock Creek, and Montgomery County was not created until 1776.

The Maryland Records[1]

In 1694, when the capital of the Province of Maryland was moved from St. Marys to Annapolis (first called "Providence," later "Anne Arundel Town"), the Assembly directed that the records should be transported to the new city on horses and in bags sealed with the Great Seal. During this removal and the long journey through deep-forest trails, many papers were greatly damaged. Others were lost in the fire of 1704, which destroyed the State House at Annapolis. In 1716, when the Government of the Province was restored to Lord Baltimore, the Assembly appointed commissioners to inspect the records and employed clerks to transcribe and bind them. It was then found that many more records were missing. Some of those records have come to light within the past year or two, in the collection of transcripts, the Colonial Records from London, now housed in the Library of Congress.

In 1882, after the turmoil of the Civil War, the Legislature of Maryland again turned its attention to the records, and passed an act directing that all the records and State papers belonging to the period prior to the Revolution be transferred to the custody of the Maryland Historical Society. The Legislature then appropriated $2,000 for the publication of extracts from these documents.

1 Abstract from J. Winsor, History of America, vol. 3.

The Virginia Records

A history of the records of the Howsing-Alexander tract is given by Chas. W. Stetson in the Records of the Columbia Historical Society, vol. 35-36, 1935, in his article "Washington's Woods on Four Mile Run." I take the liberty of repeating Mr. Stetson's statement concerning the measures used to protect the records of this grant.

"The grants of lands in the Northern Neck were recorded in large folio volumes, now stored in the Capitol building at Richmond. Considering the many removals they have undergone, it is remarkable that the series has survived in its entirety. Only a few pages are missing and a few mutilated and torn. Begun in 1690, the manuscript volumes grew to 25 before Lord Fairfax's death [1781]. Each successive agent took over the volumes containing the grants of his predecessors and added his own grants made in the name of the proprietor, but signed by himself. After he established himself in Virginia, Lord Fairfax carried the land-grant books with him over the Blue Ridge to Greenway Court where he built a small stone office for their accomodation. Greenway Court is gone, but the little office building is still standing.

"In 1785 the Legislature of Virginia passed 'An Act for the Safe Keeping of the Land Papers of the Northern Neck,' directing the removal of the land grant books to Richmond. Thereupon followed the final migration of these valuable records. They are the source books of title to some or all of the land in 19 counties of Virginia and 5 of West Virginia."

PART TWO

ORIGINAL PATENTEES AT WASHINGTON PRIOR TO 1700

On the Site Chosen in 1791 for the National Capital

At the beginning of this book is a map made in 1791 by Andrew Ellicott which is the first complete map of the District of Columbia. It was engraved in Paris by P. A. F. Tardieu in 1815, and not brought to America for many years later. Because of its authenticity, it has been used to show the location of the original land owners at Washington. The shaded covering, made by Ellicott for town sites, has been removed, and numbers inscribed on the white area to correspond with the numbers of the patentees in our list.

No. 1.   William Hutchison, owner of "The Vineyard," April 6, 1689

Hutchison's land has been described as "a rim along the Potomac and the Creek [Rock Creek]." His name appears so frequently in the early Archives of Maryland that one soon feels well acquainted with him. William Hutchison's home, "Aix," was in the lower part of Charles County, on Mattawoman Run, on the east side of a path leading from Zachia (Indian) fort to Piscataway. This estate, "laid out" for Ignatius Wheeler Jan. 4, 1687,[1] was patented to William Hutchison. Here he became well acquainted with the adjoining Piscataway Indians. Father Andrew White, a Jesuit priest, had established there a Jesuit mission in 1640, and had succeeded in teaching the Christian religion to the Emperor and his dusky family.[2]

At a meeting held in the home of Col. John Addison, who lived farther up the county on Oxon Run, the first vestry was appointed for Piscataway Parish (Episcopal) on January 30, 1693. The vestrymen appointed were John Addison, William Hatton, William Hutchison, William Taneyhill, John Emmett, and Mr. James Stodart.[3] The records of this meeting have been carefully kept to this day, and one may read in them that "John Addison, Esqr., and Mr. William Hutchison were ordered to Buy a Parcell of land att Broad Creek for ye use of ye Church."[4]

Earlier in 1693, Mr. William Hutchison, a member of the House of Burgesses for Charles County, had attended a meeting[5] to discuss the building of a free school at Annapolis,[6] and had donated 1,000 pounds of tobacco toward the project.

Later, when the Indians of Maryland moved across the Potomac and fortified themselves with the Iroquois in the mountains of Virginia, William Hutchison was commissioned to go with several other men to find out why they had left and to persuade them to return to their old fortifications in Maryland. An account of this trip is given elsewhere in this book.

Together with his friend Col. John Addison, William Hutchison acquired many acres of Maryland's virgin forests. One of these estates, "The Friendship," 1,571 acres granted in 1695, still bears its original name and is owned today by the McLean family, on Wisconsin Avenue. Years after its grant to Addison and Hutchison, it was acquired by the grandfather of Benjamin Stoddert, Col. James Stoddert, who mentions it in his will.[7]

In partnership with John Addison, Wm. Hutchison also owned "Aaron," 300 acres on the hills overlooking the mouth of Eastern Branch[8] and "White Haven," 759 acres on the hills west of Georgetown.[9] His property at the mouth of Rock Creek, called "Vineyard," was in later years acquired by Robert Peter in his patent for Mexico."[10]

1 Md. Hist. Mag. XXX, pt. 3.
2 Handbook of American Indians, Bul. 30, Bur. Ethnology, 1912.
3 Col. Records from London, vol. 724, pt. 1.
4 Piscateway Parish Records.
5 Md. Arch. vol. 19, p. 98, 1693.
6 Md. Arch. vol. 19, p. 98, 1693.
7 Wills, Pr. Georges Co., Md.; James Stoddert. Lib. 1, fol. 152, 1726.
8 Annap. Lib. 22, fol. 398.
9 Annap. Pats. BB No. 3, fol. 164.
10 U. S. vs: M. F. Morris et al. Appendix, Pt. 1, p. 121.

No. 2. **John Watson, owner of "Newbottle," Recorded 1687.**

Here is a member of the vestry of William and Mary Parish, St Marys County[1] who was true to his church is selecting a name for his patented land. "Newbottle" probably was named for an old parish in England, Newbottle, Northants, dating back to 1538.² In 1689, in an important "Address to Their Most Sacred Majesties from the Inhabitants of Charles County, Maryland," Mr. John Watson is one of the signers. The petition was for assistance for their church.³

Like Mr. William Hutchison, John Watson was generous toward the project for building a free school, in 1693, and donated 800 lbs. of tobacco.⁴ During that year his name appears as a member of the Assembly at St. Marys and a Justice of the "Provincial Court of St. Maries Citty." In 1695 we find him delegate for St. Marys⁵ and we note allowance made for his pay for 12 days' attendance as Justice in the Provincial Court, 1694, together with allowance for two days' travel, 1,840 lbs. of tobacco.

John Watson's name is shown on several of the early maps of the region in which we are interested, and as late as 1737 the location of his plantation on the Potomac between Rock Creek and the Tyber River is recorded on the map of Robert Brooke. "Newbottle" was a portion of the land acquired by Robert Peter in his patent for Mexico."⁶

The will of John Watson of St. Marys County is dated June 21, 1696, and probated April 15, 1699. (Annapolis.) Vizt:

To wife: Jane Watson, Exec., all of my estate with the exception of the bequests to the persons hereafter mentioned:

To bro. in law: Thomas Millford of St. Georges Hundred of above county, planter, one horse.

To Thomas Mitford son of said Thomas Mitford, one negro girl and her increase, also one young mare.

To Robert Graham son of Robt. Graham, dec'd., one cow and calf.

To John Greenhalgh, son of Capt. Edward Greenhalgh of St. Marys Co., Gent., Two hundred acres of land being part of a tract of land belonging to me in Prince Georges County near Rock Creek and called New bottle, to him and his heirs forever.

To Thomas Greenhalgh, son of said Capt. Greenhalgh, 100 acres of land being the rest of said tract and lying in said county, to him and his heirs forever.

                                        Jno. Watson (Seal)

Test:—

Solomon Jones; Edwd. Parsons; Edwd. Miller; Mary Miller; Jane Rose. Solomon Jones was the only witness who was not present at the probate of the above will.

Wills 6, fol. 337.

The patent for Newbottle, September 27, 1685, was given to John Watson subject to a yearly rent of 12 shillings sterling. "Granted unto John Watson of St. Marys County three hundred acres of land dated the ninth of July past—I have laid out for the said John Watson all that tract or parcell of land called Newbottle Lying in Charles County in the freshes of Potomock River beginning on the East line, with a parcell of land laid out formerly for Richard Pinner in the same County, it being the North Side of the Said Pinners Land and beginning at a bounded white Oak in a Line of the said land about half a mile from the River side and running North By East for the length of five hundred perches to a marked hicory on a branch Side of a Creek called Rock Creek then East for the Length of Ninety Six perches to a marked red oak then South by West for the length of five hundred perches to a marked red Oak in the afsd. line then with a straight Line to the first bounded Tree Now Laid out for Three hundred Acres more or less. To be held of the Mannor of Zachiah p'me Exam'd. by me Clement Hill, Dept'y Sur. Genl. Ninian Beall, Depty. Surv.

(Pats. 22, fol. 267, Annapolis)

1 Md. Arch. vol. 19, p. 3.
2 "Parish Registers of England." J. C. Cox, London. p. 14.
3 Colonial Records from London, vol. 718, pt. II.
4 Md. Arch. vol. 19, p. 98.
5 Md. Arch. vol. 19, p. 199.
6 U. S. vs: M. F. Morris et al. Appendix, pt. I, p. 121.

No. 3.   John Langworth, owner of "Widow's Mite," Oct. 10, 1664.

In the ancient description of "Widow's Mite," we find an example of a distant attempt to place the property, 600 acres "lying on the east side of the Anacostin River [meaning the Potomac] on the north side of a branch or inlett in the said river called Tyber."[1]

John Langworth came to America in 1637/8 indentured to Thomas Gerrard.[2] His brother James Langworth arrived in Maryland in 1658.[3] It was the son, William, of James, who so made his will, in 1693/4, that we learn more about "Widow's Mite." To his wife Ann, William Langworth leaves his plantation, 150 acres, and 150 acres called "Mills Marsh." To his daughter Agatha, 240 acres "Highpark;" to his daughter Elizabeth, 120 acres "St. Barbaries Addition;" to his daughter Mary and her heirs, residue of land in St. Mary's County. Evidently there were no sons, and the daughters were content with their lot, for the 600 acres of "Widow's Mite," were ordered to be sold.[4]

In 1692, when St. Marys County was divided into two parishes, New Town Hundred and Clements Hundred were divided[5] by "Mr. Langworth's Branch" which led to the Patuxent main road, thus marking the location of William and Mary Parish on the lower side and King and Queen Parish on the upper.[6]

Evidently the Langworth family moved up into Charles County, for in 1666, during trouble with Indians, "Mrs. Langworth's children" were killed, and when the murderers were captured and one Indian killed by the English, it was found that the killing took place "at the head of Port Tobacco Creek upon Colonel (Gerard) Fowke's land about a week after the murder of Mrs. Langworth's children."[7]

"Widow's Mite" extended northward from Tyber to "a bounded oke the bound tree of Richard Pinner" and then on over the area later the city to a point just north of what is now 18th Street and Columbia Road.[8]

1 Annap. Rec. Lib. 10, fol. 528.
2 List of Early Settlers, Lib. Congress; also Annap. ABH fol. 101.
3 List of Early Settlers, Lib. Congress; also Annap. Q, fol. 19.
4 Md. Cal. Wills, vol. 2, p. 69.
5 Md. Arch. vol. 8, p. 235; also, Skirven, P. G., "First Parishes of the Province of Maryland."
6 Md. Arch. vol. 23, p. 17, 1692.
7 Md. Arch. vol. 23.
8 Lib. 10, fol. 528. Annap.

No. 4.   John Lewger, owner of "Layton Stone", previous to 1666.

Secretary John Lewger! The Archives of Maryland fairly ring with his history. He was born in London in 1602. Admitted to Trinity College in Oxford, 1616, and graduated 1619. Converted to the Catholic Church, but returned to Protestantism in 1634. He arrived in Maryland in 1637, where he was given the duties of Secretary of the Province, Registrar of the Land Office, Collector of Customs, and Receiver of Quit Rents.[1] In addition, he was a member of the Privy Council, Justice for conservation of the Peace, and on Sept. 5, 1642, Councillor, Judge of all Causes Testamentary and Matrimonial, Principal Officer and Keeper of the Acts and Proceedings, etc.[2] Is it any wonder, therefore, that he neglected to register his patent for "Layton Stone," located on Tyber River between Pinner's "Father's Gift" and Langworth's "Widow's Mite"? The only record of Layton Stone available at Annapolis is in the patent for "Father's Gift."[3]

In the records at Annapolis there is recorded, however, that Martha Lewger, in 1668, was the widow of John Lewger,[4] and that the will of John Lewger of Charles County was filed in 1669.[5]

In the days of Maryland history when Giles Brent was Acting Governor of Maryland while Leonard Calvert visited in Europe, in June, 1644, Secretary Lewger gave a commission to Henry Fleet to treat with the Piscataway Indians for the conclusion of peace. Acting Governor Brent, deeming that he had overstepped his powers, suspended him, August 26, 1644, from his office and revoked all commissions granted him. In the bright days of September, however, Leonard Calvert returned and Mr. Lewger was not only restored to office but was given additional powers. It was then that he was made Secretary of the Province, Attorney General, Judge of Causes etc., Register of the Land Office, and member of the Council.

In the Maryland Archives[6] is the interesting record that Richard Lee willed to Mrs. Lewger "a sattin petticoate w'ch was his wives, worth 10 lb." This will was witnessed by "John Lewger, Secy."

---

1 Streeter Papers, 1876, p. 104, Md. Hist. Soc.
2 Md. Arch. ol. 3, p. 114.
3 Annap. Rec., Lib. 10, fol. 284.
4 Annap. Rec., Lib. 12, fol. 502.
5 Annap. Wills, Lib. 1, fol. 356.
6 Md. Arch. vol. 4, p. 51.

No. 5. Richard and William Pinner, owners of "Fathers' Gift," Oct. 11, 1666.

Richard Pinner, father of Richard and William, came to Maryland in 1638, indentured.[1] From the Eastern Shore, vicinity of Elizabeth River, Va.,[2] he came to Charles County to live, and there settled and died.[3] There is record in that county of a tract called "Pinner"[4] which in 1718 was purchased by Dr. Gustavus Brown of Port Tobacco.

Richard Pinner had a warrant for land due him for transporting himself and his wife, his sons Richard and William, and for Christopher Brome, Roger Cordin, Ellinor and Elizabeth Jefreys, Martha and Maud, and Dina, a Negro.[5] He died, however, without taking up this warrant, leaving it to his sons as his heritage. In 1666, therefore, the sons Richard and William received patent for "Father's Gift," 500 acres, "lying on the east side of the Anacostin [Potomac] River on the north side of a branch in the said river called Tyber that respecteth the land of Francis Pope called Rome bounding on the south with the said Tyber river from a bounded oke being the bound tree of the land of John Lewger called Layton Stone - - -."[6]

In 1685[7] William Pinner, planter, of Charles County, made his will, leaving to his mother Ann Atkins (Pinner), all that tract of land she now lives on, 300 acres. to his brother Richard Pinner he leaves his two cows. But previous to the making of this will, Richard had made his own will in 1684.[8] He had two daughters, Anna and Elizabeth, to whom he devised "all my land being 300 acres to be divided between them after the death of their mother, my wife Mary Pinner." It would seem, therefore, that both wills were made previous to death, and that "Fathers Gift" had been divided between the brothers. Neither will mentioned a son, and the name evidently there ended. From this will we gain the interesting information that the mother of the boys, Ann Atkins Pinner, was actually living in this region in 1685.[9]

1 List of Early Settlers, Lib. Cong. Also, Annap. ABH, fol. 37, 64.
2 Allen C. Clark, "Orig. of the Fed. City," p. 85, 1935.
3 Annap. Pat. II, fol. 351.
4 Chas. Co., Md. Lib. H No. 2, fol. 191, 1718. 7 Annap. Wills, June 17, 1685.
5 Annap. Pat. II, fol. 351.   8 Annap. Wills, Feb. 1, 1684.
6 Annap. Lib. 10, fol. 284; Lib. 11, fol. 351. 9 Annap. Wills, June 17, 1685.

**No. 6. John Peerce, owner of "Jamaica" and of "Port Royal,"
Sept. 23, 1685.**

Here is a name for ancient spellers to "conjure with."
One finds it spelled "Peerce," "Pearce," or "Pierce," yet
we have comparatively little of his history. His patent
states that he is of Calvert County, and it further enlightens by
adding that his land is "in the freshes of potomoke River near
the head of a Creek called Broad Creek," meaning in the
freshes of Potomac River near the head of Tyber Creek.

John Peerce (or Pearce) is not listed among the early
settlers of Maryland, most of this honor falling to "Coll. Wil-
liam Pierce (also Pearce)," who settled Oct. 15, 1697, in Cecil
County, Maryland, and was vestryman on the south side of
Sassafrasse Parish.[1] There also is recorded a "Pearces ffolley"
surveyed for Wm. Pearce July 16, 1716, lying in Baltimore
County, in woods between Patapsco Falls and Gunpowder
Falls.[2] William Pearce was transported prior to 1666.[3]

On the map of J. M. Toner and S. R. Seibert, 1874, Port
Royal and Jamaica, each of 500 acres more or less, are shown
extending north and eastward across the site of Washington
from the White House area to the city's boundary, and touch-
ing on the northeast the upper branches of the Tiber.

The old Pearce (or Peerce) homestead, referred to by Gen-
eral Washington in his descriptive outlines of the new Federal
City[4] was situated on the north side of what is now Pennsyl-
vania Avenue opposite the White House, at Lafayette Park.
The mansion and its family lived during the Eighteenth
Century, however, and are recorded by Christian Hines and by
Allen C. Clark.[5]

For John Peirce of Calvert Co., September 23, 1685:
Port Royal. 500 Acres.

"Land called port Royall lying in Charles County in the
freshes of potomoke River near the head of a Creek called
Broad Creek (head of Tiber Creek) beginning at a marked
white oak within half a mile of the head of the said Creek and
running east by north for the length of 500 p. to a bounded
hiccory then north for the length of 160 p. to marked red oak
then west by south for the length of 500 p. to a marked white
oak then with a straight line to the first bounded tree."

Annap. Lib. 22, fol. 276; Pat. NS No. 2, fol. 310-330.

Jamaica. 500 Acres.

"Tract called Jamaica lying in Charles County in the freshes of potomock River and on the north side of a creek called broad Creek beginning at a bounded white oak of the aforesaid Peirces land runing east by north for the length of five hundred perches to a marked red oak then north for the length of one hundred and sixty perches to a marked white oak then west by south for the length of five hundred perches to a marked red oak then with a straight line to the first bounded tree now laid out for five hundred acres more or less."

Annap. Lib. 22, fol. 268; Pat. NS No. 2, fol. 310.

---

1 Col. Records from London. 5, vol. 724, pt. I.
2 Md. Hist. Mag. vol. 30, Pt. 2, p. 136.
3 Annap. Lib. 10, fol. 417; also List of Early Settlers, Lib. Congress.
4 Washington's Letter, 1791, to Deakins and Stoddert. U. S. vs: M. F. Morris
    et al. Record 7, vol. 5, p. 2168.
5 Allen C. Clark, "Origin of the Federal City," p. 88, 1935.

No. 7.   Francis Pope, owner of "Rome" on the Tyber, June 5, 1663.

In the early records at Annapolis, one finds:
ffrancis Pope, transported since 1635; wife 1649.[1]
And in the Proceedings of the early Assemblies:
ffrancis Pope—member of the Assembly in September, 1642,[2] and 1667 and 1670, he was Justice of the Peace for Charles County, Maryland.[3]

In an old volume of precious records at Annapolis, Liber 6, folio 318: "June 5th, 1663, Layd out for Francis Pope of this Province, Gent., a parcel of land in Charles County called Rome, lying on the East side of the Anacostian River[4] [meaning here, the main channel of the Potomac], **beginning at a marked oak standing by the River side, the bounded tree of Captain Robert Troop** and running north by the river for breadth the length 200 perches to a bounded oak standing at the mouth of a bay or inlet called Tiber, bounding on the north by the said Lett and a line drawn east for the length of 320 perches to a bounded oak standing in the woods on the East with a line drawn south from the end of the former line until you meet with the exterior bounded tree of **Robert Troop called Scotland Yard** on the south with the said land, on the west with the said river (Tyber), containing and now laid out for 400 acres more or less."

Capt. Robert Troop's "Scotland Yard," itself north of the tract "New Troy" which extended far north of the Capitol[5] and Congressional Library of today, was therefore the southern boundary of Mr. Pope's Rome.

Yet, about 150 years later, in 1804, Tom Moore, the poet, 25 years of age, spent "near a week" with Mr. and Mrs. Merry, the family of the early English minister, in Washington. Later, in a note to his Epistle to Thomas Hume, Moore gave his ideas of the infant city, and then wrote the following rhyme on the Capitol City of that date.

> "In fancy, now, beneath the twilight gloom,
> Come, let me lead thee o'er the second Rome
> Where tribunes rule, where dusky Davi bow,
> And what was Goose creek once is Tiber now;
> This embryo Capital, where fancy sees
> Squares in morasses, obelisks in trees
> Which second-sighted seers, even now adorn
> With shrines unbuilt and heroes yet unborn."[6]

Moore writes of the **Capital**, not the **Capitol!** Perhaps he had never heard of Francis Pope, for certainly he would have mentioned "the Pope at Rome," or something to that effect in his verses. Yet, the popular interpretation has rolled on through the years, and many followers of the romantic now actually are convinced that Pope's "Rome" was on the site where our Nation's Capitol Building now stands.

In the Manuscript Division of the Library of Congress, a set of original papers of the Bozeman family give interesting information regarding John Pope of "Rome," his wife Margaret, his brother Robert, and his **daughter Frances.** The will of John Pope, dated 1702, is given, as follows:

> "I give and bequeath unto my loving brother Robert Pope, if living at my decease, the sum of 10 pounds sterling, to be paid by my executors within convenient time after my decease; but if my said brother should not then be living, my will is that my said executors pay the said sum of 10 Pounds sterling to the next heir of the said Robert Pope, and to him or her to hold and enjoy forever.

"Item. All the rest of my estate, both real and
personal, I give and bequeath to my dear and loving
wife, Margaret Pope, and to her heirs and assigns
forever. But if it should so happen that my said wife
marry or depart this life without any disposition of
the said estate, then my will is that after my said
wife's decease, the same shall go and descend to my
daughter Frances Ungle, and to the heir of her body
begotten or to be begotten forever, and for want of
said issue, then I give and bequeath the same estate
to my aforesaid brother Robert Pope, near Bristol in
the Kingdom of England, and to his heirs and assigns forever."

                                              John Pope.

There is a following notation made by C. N. Goldsborough
in 1763 regarding the application of this will. It is noted that
Margaret Pope never married again, but sold part of the real
estate and mortgaged the rest. Goldsborough adds: "What
estate had Mrs. Pope in the land called Rome under the will
of her husband John Pope?" and "What estate had Mrs. Ungle
in the land? She was Frances, the daughter of John Pope,
mentioned in his will. Mrs. Pope had undoubtedly an estate
in fee simple in the land called Rome under the will of her
husband, etc."

Then follows the notation: "She (Mrs. Pope) sold her
Lotts in Oxford to Mrs. Ungle and the land called Rome she
mortgaged, for 100 pounds Sterl. to be paid at the end of six
years, without any express stipulation for interest; on the day
of the signing of the mortgage an agreement signed by Mr.
Grundy, the Mortgager, was made, expressing that Mrs.
Grundy was to have the use of the land six years and at the
expiration of that time to restore it to Mrs. Pope. Whether
the use of the land was for the interest of the money only, or
for the Principal and interest, does not appear by any writing
that has come to my hands. The original mortgage was found
among Mrs. Ungle's papers, which shows that it had been giv-
en up by Mr. Grundy or by Mr. Lloyd his executor. Mrs. Pope
never could have paid 100 pounds sterling. She borrowed it
to enable her to go to England, in hopes of recovering her Eye
sight, and was so needy after she returned that Mrs. Ungle
chiefly supported her; I see by a letter from Mrs. Ungle to
my father in 1722 that Mrs. Ungle had then thought of selling

the land, so that it may reasonably be supposed that the mortgage to Mr. Grundy was discharged.

"Query: Is this act of Mrs. Pope's such a disposition as will defeat that part of John Pope's will which limits it to his brother Robert Pope and his heirs?"

Further investigation might prove that John Pope,[7] in Oxford Town, Talbot County, Maryland, was related to the original patentee of Rome, Francis Pope, who arrived in Maryland "since 1635," and that John Pope had named his only child, his daughter Frances, for her grandfather(?) Francis Pope. If it be true that Francis Pope of Rome died and left his property to John Pope of Oxford, and that the "Rome" mentioned in the grant of 1663 to Francis Pope and in the will of 1702 of John Pope are the same place, then can we understand why the name "Rome" faded away from the area of the National Capital in so complete a manner, leaving only the romantic verses written later by Mr. Moore.

1 Annap. ABH 23, 24, 95.
2 Md. Archives, vol. 1, p. 176.
3 Assembly Proceedings, vol. 15, 1667.
4 "Anacostine River" refers to the main channel of the Potomac.
5 Annap. Lib. 6, fol. 174.
6 Townsend, Geo. Alfred, "Washington Outside and Inside," 1873. p. 551.
7 Md Arch. vol. 8, p. 560, 562.—"In Oxford Town at the house of Mr. John Pope, 1693."

No. 8.   Robert Troope, owner of "Scotland Yard," June 5, 1663.

Lieutenant Robert Troope was an immigrant in 1651.[1] Through his bravery and his services at Severn, he received a special warrant for land, from Lord Baltimore.[2] His grant for "Scotland Yard" was one of the earliest land grants in this region. It was mentioned in the grant to George Thompson for "New Troy," dated February 12, 1663.

"Laid out for Capt. Robert Troop of this Province a parcell of land in Charles County called Scotland Yard lying on the East side of the Anacostine River,[3] Beginning at a bounded hickary standing by the Water side, and running North up the River, for breadth the length of Two hundred and fifty perches, to a bounded Oak bounding on the North with a Line

drawn East into the woods for the length of Three
hundred and twenty perches, to a bounded Oak on the
East with a line drawn South from the end of the
former line until you intersect a parralell Line drawn
from the first bounded hikary on the South with the
said parralell, on the West, with the said River, Containing and now laid out for five hundred acres more
or less.

John Lewger, Depty. Sur.
Pats. 6, fol. 333-334. Annapolis.

---

1 Early Settlers in Maryland, Lib. Congress.
2 Annap. Lib. 4, fol. 584.
3 In this case, as in many others in the early land grants, the main branch
  of the Potomac River is called "the Anacostine River," probably because
  of the Anacostine Indians who lived on both shores.

No. 9. George Thompson, owner of 3 tracts, "Duddington Mannor," "Duddington Pasture," and "New Troy," Feb. 12, 1663.

Far back in the Old Country, in Somerset, was Doddington
Manor, the home of the Doddingtons, who were relatives of
the Thompsons in England.[1] Perhaps it was for this reason
that George Thompson named his enormous holdings along
the Potomac River and the Eastern Branch, or Anacostia
River. It was the first patent granted by Lord Baltimore for
land in this region and was obtained by Special Warrant of
October, 1662,[2] composed of 1,000 acres from Lord Baltimore,
"Duddington Mannor," 500 acres, "New Troy," by warrant
allowed Thomas Hussey, Gent., and 300 acres, "Duddington
Pasture," from John Lewger, Gent., assignee of Thomas Gerrard, Gent., being part of a warrant of 400 acres granted said
Gerrard.[3]

At the time Charles County was organized, 1658, George
Thompson was Clerk of the County Court.[4] On June 1, 1668,
he was at St. Marys, an attorney for Raymond Stapleford in
his case against Jo. Balley.[5] As late as 1691, his name appears
in connection with Notley Hall.[6] On Nov. 9, 1670, George
Thompson leased, for 1,000 years, his tracts to his friend,
Thomas Notley, who patented them March, 1, 1671, under the
new name "Cerne Abbey Manor,"[7] a name dear to his boyhood.
In old Dorset, he had spent many of his young days at the

Manor of Cerne Abbey, which had farms belonging to the
Abbot of Cerne.[8] Notley belonged to the illustrious family of
Sydenhams of Coombe, Dorset, who were nobles in 1275.[9] His
coming to America is said to be coincident with that of Charles
Calvert, his friend in London. From 1676 until his death three
years later, Notley was Deputy Governor of Maryland. During
this period he had disposed of nearly all his landed estates,
Charles Lord Baltimore being in almost every instance the
purchaser. Thus the Proprietary became owner of the cele-
brated country seat, Notley Hall, on the Wicomico River.[10]
By the will of Thomas Notley, April 3, 1679, Cerne Abbey
Manor is left to his godson, Notley Rozier, son of Benjamin
Rozier and his wife Anne Sewall, daughter of the second wife
of Charles Calvert. It has been recorded that Notley Rozier
was reared by his grandmother, Lady Baltimore, at Notley
Hall, the estate of his godfather and benefactor.[11]

Notley Rozier married Jane Digges, who brought to her
husband a dower of 1,000 acres across the Anacostia River,
known as Elizabeth. Their daughter, Ann Rozier, married Daniel Carroll, second son of Charles Carroll, immigrant and Attorney General. Ann Rozier Carroll was widowed
while still a young woman, and married Col. Benjamin Young,
the Commissioner of Crown Lands, who came to Maryland
about 1735.[12] Thus Ann Rozier Carroll Young was known as
the heiress of Notley Hall and also of Cerne Abbey Manor.
In addition, she owned Giesboro and Blue Plains across the
Anacostia River, which Gov. Thomas Notley had purchased
from George Thompson in 1670, and Elizabeth, 1,000 acres
of wooded land above the Anacostia River and the Potomac,
which had come to her father, Notley Rozier, by his marriage
with Jane Digges.

However, Cerne Abbey Manor had experienced a change
of name in 1716, when Notley Rozier had obtained for it his
patent "Duddington Manor," the original name for the property. At this time parts of waste land were excluded and new
land was added.[13] Thus it came to his daughter, who was
twice married and had sons, Charles Carroll and Notley Young.
Daniel Carroll, son of Charles, and Notley Young were the
last manorial owners of this vast tract which covered Capitol
Hill, Southwest Washington, the Navy Yard, Southeast Wash-

ington, and a large tract north of the Capitol and the Congressional Library of today.[14]

Here is the Supreme Court (Dist. of Col.) version of the ownership of the Duddington tracts:

U. S. vs. M. F. Morris et al. Record 7, vol. 5.

Evidence

Page 2135:

Charter from the Crown of England to Coecilius Calvert, Baron of Baltimore, June 20, 1632.

Patent from the Colonial authorities of Maryland, Feb. 12, 1633, to George Thompson for tracts of land called Duddington Manor, Duddington Pasture, and New Troy.

Deed of lease for 1,000 years for same property, Nov. 20, 1670, from George Thompson to Thomas Notley.

Patent from the Colonial authorities of Maryland, March 1, 1671, to Thomas Notley for the same property on a resurvey by the name of Cerne Abbey Manor.

Thomas Notley's last will and testament dated April 2, 1678, and approved April 3, 1678, devising said land to Notley Rozier in fee.

Patent from the Colonial authorities of Maryland, September 10, 1716, to Notley Rozier for 1536 acres under the name of Duddington Manor granted on a warrant to resurvey said tracts called New Troy, Duddington Manor and Duddington Pasture, leaving out certain barren land.

It is stipulated and agreed between Solicitors that said Notley Rozier inter-married with Jane Digges and that title to said land passed by deeds of lease and release by way of marriage settlement dated the 1st and 2nd of Feb. 1702, from Notley Rozier to Edward Digges and Anthony Neill, and that Eleanor Rozier the only child of the marriage of Notley Rozier and Jane Digges, married Daniel Carroll, and that title passed to Charles Carroll of Duddington, who was the only son of the marriage aforesaid, and from him to his eldest son Daniel Carroll, and from said Daniel last mentioned to his eldest son, Charles Carroll Jr., by descent.

Deed of lease for one year, Aug. 17, 1758, from Charles Carroll to Ann Young, of 400 acres, part of the land patented to Notley Rozier as aforesaid.

Deed of release, Aug. 18, 1758, from Charles Carroll, to Ann Young, of said last mentioned property.
Surveyed and plat of resurvey of Cerne Manor, May 16, 1759.
Patent from the Colonial authorities of Maryland, Jan. 8, 1760, to Charles Carroll of the land included in said last mentioned resurvey.
Deed from Ann Young to Notley Young, Dec. 5, 1761. (It is agreed between the Solicitors that the tract of Notley Young extended from a point at the junction of the Anacostia River or Eastern Branch with the Potomac River known as Greenleaf Point or the Arsenal Point, to a point above the Long Bridge and including all the squares along the river to and including No. 233.)
Deed from Notley Young, June 28, 1791, to Thomas Beall of George and John Mackall Gantt conveying all interest in lands within a certain limits which include the said tract of 400 acres, in trust, to be laid out for the Federal City.

1 Margaret Brent Downing. Col. Hist. Soc., vol. 21, 1918.
2 Pat No. 6, fol. 174, Annap.
3 Pat. No. 6, fol. 174, Annap.
4 Md. Hist. Soc. Rec. of Early Chas. Co.
5 Md. Arch., vol. 2, p. 379.
6 Md. Arch., vol. 8, p. 259, 1691.
7 U. S. vs: M. F. Morris et al, Record 7, vol. 5.
8 Margaret Brent Downing, Col. Hist Soc., vol. 21, 1918.
9 Margaret Brent Downing, Col. Hist. Soc., vol. 21, 1918.
10 Margaret Brent Downing, Col. Hist. Soc., vol. 21, 1918.
11 Margaret Brent Downing, Col. Hist. Soc., vol. 21, 1918.
12 Margaret Brent Downing, Col. Hist. Soc., vol. 21, 1918.
13 U. S. vs: M. F. Morris et al. Rec. vol. 6, 1887, fol. 379 and 382.
14 M. B. Downing, Col. Hist. Soc. vol. 21, 1918.

No. 10. Walter Houp, owner of 'Houp Yard," July 20, 1686.

The name of this family has been spelled in various ways: Houp, Hope, Hoape, and Hop.
In 1665, Richard Hope was transported to Maryland.[1] In 1686, Walter Houp patented "Houp Yard."[2] In 1689, Mr. Henry Houp was appointed "to regulate Civill Affairs in Dorchester County, Maryland."[3]
On the map of Cerne Abbey Manor made by J. F. A. Priggs in 1793 for Charles Carroll, the notation is made that "Houp Yard" immediately joined it on the east, according to the resurvey in 1759.

The certificate to Walter Houp for 500 acres called "Houp Yard, fronting on the Eastern Branch," stipulates that it is adjoined on the east by the Walter Thompson lands, and is dated July 20, 1686.[4]

1 Annap. Lib. 7, fol. 560.
2 Annap. Lib. 22, fol. 240.
3 Col. Records from London, vol. 718, pt. I, 1689.
4 Lib. 22, fol. 240, Annapolis.

No. 11. Walter Thompson, owner of "The Nock." Feb. 16. 1686

Warrant granted unto Ninian Beall of Calvert County for 500 acres of land dated 11th September last past unto sd. Beall and by assignment from sd. Beall to Walter Thompson of Calvert County for the whole warrant of 500 acres dated 11th September last past. I Ninian Beall have laid out for sd. Thompson all that tract of land called the Nock lying in Charles County and on the North side of the Eastern Branch of Potomack River and beginning at the branch side at a white oak it being the South West corner tree of a parcell of land laid out for Andrew Clarke, and running North North West for the length of 500 perches to a marked white oak by the side of a small branch then West South West for the length of 160 perches to a marked white oak by a pecoson side then South South East for the length of 500 perches to a marked hiccory by the River side, then with a straight line to the first bounded tree, now laid out for 500 acres more or less. To be held of the Mannor of Zachiah.

p me Ninian Beall Depty. Sur.
(Patents 22, fol. 214. Annapolis)

According to the certificate to Walter Houp for "Houp Yard," the Walter Thompson land, "The Nock," adjoined it on the east.

No. 12. Andrew Clarke, owner of "Meurs," Sept. 24, 1685.

September the 24th, 1685. By virtue of a Warr't granted unto Ninian Beall bearing date the 14th day of July last past for five hundred acres of land and by Assignment from the said Beall unto Andrew Clarke of Calv't. County, Merchant by virtue thereof I have laid out for the said Clarke all that tract or parcell of land called Meurs lying in Charles County on the North side of Eastern Branch of Potomack. Containing five hundred acres. To be held of the Mannor of Zachaia per me Ninian Beale, Dept'y. Sur. A true Cert. examined by me Clement Hill, D. Sur. Gen'l.

(Patents 22, fol. 268.
Patents N. S. No. 2, fol. 353.)

According to a later land grant (1733, to Thomas Evans, Pat. A. M. No. 1, fol. 397) Clarke died without heirs and the property, "Meurs," became escheat to Lord Baltimore. Later, in 1733, Thomas Evans, the grandson of Emigrant Ninian Beall, took out a patent. The land had been issued to Ninian Beall in 1700, March 10, however, patented under the name "Chance" (D. D. 38)—"beginning at a branch called Cabbin Branch adjoining Walltor Evans' land, 132 acres."—Possibly this was merely a portion of the original tract "Meurs."

No. 13. Zachariah Wade, owner of "Brothers Purchase," July 16, 1670

Mr. "Zachary" Wade, as he is referred to in the Archives of Maryland, was an attorney at St. Marys as early as 1648, during which year he gave evidence in the case of a stolen "Red Cow" which had been presented by the "late Governor deceased" to Captain Vaughn.[1]

In 1650, he was attorney for Thomas Bradnock of the Isle of Kent, who brought to the court at St. Marys his troubles with Edward Hudson, age 25 years, who claimed that he had hidden (for security) "in the Corne Loft of Mr. Bradnock a parcell of peese, a Kacke of Sope, and also a bottell of Vinegar, also a parcell of Shott."[2]

On January 2, 1665, in the Assembly at St. Marys, the following persons were chosen by unanimous consent to serve as Burgesses for Charles County:

Mr. Zachary Wade, Capt. James Neale, Coll. Gerard ffowke, Mr. Thomas Thurrowgood.

In March, 1675, Mr. Zachary Wade and Mr. ffrancis Pope were named Justices of the Peace for Charles County.[3]

Zachary Wade's patent of 780 acres, "Brothers Purchase," was taken up, with Capt. Luke Gardner, July 16, 1670.—"A

parcell of land lying in the woods above Piscattaway called
Brothers Purchase in Charles County (now Prince Georges
County) beginning at a bounded white oak standing upon a
plain running thence South South West 140 perches to a
bounded white oak standing by the branch side—binding upon
the said branch South South East 70 perches to a bounded
white oak thence East 110 perches to a bounded Chestnutt
standing by a deep branch—thence West by South 165 perches
to a bounded white oak thence until it comes to the first bound
tree Containing and now laid out for 780 Acres. To be held
of Zachaia."

Richard Edelen, Depty. Sur.
(Pat. 19, fol. 570, Annapolis).

1 Md. Arch. 4, p. 394-395.
2 Md. Arch. 2 (Assembly Proc.) page 50, 1649-50.
3 Md. Arch. 15 (Assembly Proc.) page 68.

No. 14.   Richard Evans, owner of "Barbadoe," March 30, 1685.

The land of Mr. Richard Evans, acquired 1685, was adjoined in 1698 by Walter Evans' new "Nameless."[1]

In the Annapolis list of early Maryland settlers, Richard
Evans is recorded as the son of Obediah Evans, and transported 1667.[2]

Although his warrant came by way of Col. Henry Dar-
nell,[3] Richard Evans of Calvert County patented his "Barba-
doe" after it was "Laid out"for him by Ninian Beall, Deputy
Surveyor, in Charles County, on the West side of the Eastern
branch of Potomack River beginning at a marked White Oak
by a Small branch Side on the East side of sd. branch—containing and laid out for 250 acres more or less."[4] His rent to
Lord Baltimore for this grant was ten shillings Sterling,
Yearly.

The "White Oak by a Small branch Side" in later years
and future deeds became historic. This is the stream referred to by Ninian Beall as "Cabbin Branch" in this area,

and later owned with its famous spring by Major Benjamin Stoddert.

1 Annap. Pat. CC No. 4, fol. 353.
2 Annap. Lib. 18, fol. 314.
3 A number of land grants on the Washington area were made through warrants issued to Colonel Henry Darnall, who was perhaps the "largest land" holder in this region. "Gyrles' Portion," one of his vast holdings, originally extended from the north of Washington's boundry to Forest Glenn and Silver Spring, taking in what is now Rock Creek Park and Walter Reed Hospital. A portion of this land was in later years purchased by the carroll family.
4 Annap. Lib. 22, fol. 164.

No. 15.   William Atcheson, tract unamed.   1698 (or previous)

William Atcheson, whose patent for this tract has not been located, was in later years owner of several other tracts. In this locality, his land is referred to in the grant for Walter Evans' "Nameless."[1] It is possible that his tract, like a number of others on the Eastern Branch (or Anacostia River) was obtained through the transfer of a warrant issued to Col. Ninian Beall, who was Deputy Surveyor.

After 1700, William Atcheson took out patents for three tracts in Charles County, as follows:

Atchisons Woodyard, 100 acres, on the north side of the Piney Branch of Mattawoman,[2] 1714.

Atchison's Hazzard, 100 acres in Charles County near the land of Henry Acton called Aberdeen and adjoining his own land formerly taken up,[3] 1725.

Grub Street, 86 acres,[4] 1727.

1 Pat. E. E. No. 6, fol. 58, 59, Annapolis.
2 Pat. E. E. No. 6, fol. 58, 59.
3 Pat. I. L. No. A, fol. 609, Annapolis.
4 Pat. I. L. No. A, fol. 702, Annapolis.

No. 16.   Walter Evans, owner of "Nameless", Dec. 9, 1698.

The name "Evans in connection with the Eastern Branch of the Potomac brings to light a family who lived in the vicinity many years and in time left their name geographically, at Evans Point.

There is record that Walter Evans was taxed for "ex-

penses of the Government," in 1681, 220 lbs. of tobacco, and
in 1682, his tax rose to 4,800 lbs. of the weed.[1]

In 1692, Walter Evans was one of the 11 brave men
selected to serve under Capt. Richard Brightwell as Rangers
for Scotland Hundred.[2]

In 1698, Walter Evans was granted 230 acres on the Eastern Branch of the Potomac, by courtesy of Col. Ninian Beall,
who had warrant for 1,000 acres of land at that time. The
tract was patented to Walter Evans December 9 under the odd
name "Nameless." Three neighbors are mentioned in the deed,
Richard Evans, Zachariah Wade, and William Atcheson, each
of whom had owned their adjoining tracts many years previous to Walter Evans' patent of "Nameless."[3]

Walter Evans' will,[4] filed in Prince Georges County, is
dated 1731. His son, Walter Evans, "on the Eastern Branch,"
was taxed for remaining a bachelor "aged 25 years and upwards" in 1756, when the Maryland Assembly, needing funds
for the French and Indian War, called on the vestry of Rock
Creek Church to ascertain and certify such bachelors.[5]

There is record of Walter Evans' marriage, however, to
Elizabeth Beall, born 1743, daughter of Ninian Beall's son
Col. George Beall and his wife Elizabeth Brooke.[6]

---

1 Md. Arch. ol. 7, p. 251, 441.
2 Md. Arch. vol. 8, p. 445.
3 Pat. C. C. No. 4, fol. 144. Dec. 9, 1698. Annapolis.
4 Annap. Wills; Lib. 20, fol. 203.
5 Md. Arch., Acts of Assembly, 1756. Also Browne, A. S. Col Hist. Soc. Rec.
   vol. 9.
6 "Col. Families of the U. S." Mackenzie, C. N. vol. II, p. 57.

No. 17.   Col. Henry Jowles, owner of "The Grange," Feb. 25, 1685.

Colonel Henry Jowles was in charge of the Militia of the
Province of Maryland in 1682.[1] In 1689 he received 20,000
lbs. of tobacco as a gift for his services in raising troops for
the defence of the Province.[2] On the 25th of August, 1689,
Colonel Jowles sent information to the President and Council
then in session at St. Marys, that 3,000 Indians were at the
head of the Patuxent River, marching toward the interior
settlements, and he begged that the inhabitants be furnished

with arms and ammunition for their protection. On receipt of
this information, the Council immediately despatched Col.
Digges with the necessary arms.

On April 10, 1685, the following grant of land was made.
"By virtue of a War't. of 500 Acres of land granted to Col.
Henry Jowles of Calvert County the 25th day of February last
past, I have laid out for the said Jowles all that tract or parcel
of land called The Grange Lying in Charles County on the
North side of the Eastern Branch of Potomock River, containing 500 acres. To be held of the Mannor of Zachia per me
Ninian Beale, Dept'y. Sur. A true Cert. examined by me Clement Hill, D. Sur. Gen'l.[3]

The following communication, dated March 2, 1695, is of
interest.

> "Whereas by a late commission granted to us
> and our Royal Consort Queen Mary lately dec'd, dated
> ye 14th of May last (1694), Coll. Henry Jowles Esq.,
> was instituted Chiefe Judge in Chancery and Keeper
> of our Great Seal of Maryland—and whereas ye said
> Coll. Henry Jowles Esq. being at present afflicted with
> ye Gout and other Indispositions of body, is therefore
> unable to attend ye sd. Court of Chancery and ye
> Causes, and our said Court require dispatch and can-
> not without public prejudice be delayed—Know Ye
> yet We have therefore assigned you ye sd. Coll.
> Nicho. Greenbury, Kenelm Cheseldyne and Major
> Edw. Dorsey, Esqs., commissioners and judges of our
> High Court of Chancery in our said Province of Mary-
> land untill such time as ye above said Coll. Henry
> Jowles—shall be able to attend his said office to keep
> and cause to be kept all Ordinances, etc." - -[4]

In the will[5] of Coll. Henry Jowles, dated Sept. 19, 1695,
and probated Feb. 17, 1700, he leaves the plantation "where
now I live, called Johns Dorp" to his son Henry Jowles; to his
daughter Rebecca, all that tract of land called "The Grange"
lying on the Eastern Branch of Potomuck in Charles County
now called Prince Georges County, containing 500 acres, to
have same when 18 years of age or on day of marriage. If
she die to her sister Sybell, and if she die to my son Henry
Jowles."

A corner of The Grange came within the bounds of the National Capital when the city was surveyed by Washington and

his talented Engineer, Maj. L'Enfant, in 1791. It was near the toll gate which in 1866 stood at the junction of Bladensburg Road and the Boundary, now Florida Avenue.

1 Md. Arch. vol. 5, p. 353-354.
2 Scharf, Hist. of Md., vol. I, p. 307.
3 Annapolis, Pat. 22, fol. 166, and N. S. No. 2 fol. 91.
4 Chancery Proc., Lib. P. C. No. 2, fol. 320.
5 Col. Wills, vol. 2, Annap. vol. 6, fol. 399.

No. 18. Col. Ninian Beall, owner of "Inclosure," Oct. 2, 1687.

The whole life of Ninian Beall was colorful. He was born in Largo, Fifeshire, Scotland, in 1625. He held a commission as cornetist in the Scotch-English Army raised to resist Cromwell, and fought and was made prisoner in the battle of Dunbar, September 3, 1650. Sentenced to five years of servitude, he was sent with 150 other Scotchmen to Barbadoes, West Indies. About 1652 he appeared in Maryland[1] and served his five years servitude with Richard Hall, a planter of Calvert County. There is a court record of his making a land transfer in the county in 1658. (Lib. 5, fol. 416, Md. Land Office.)

Ninian Beall received his freedom in 1667, at which time he proved his right to 50 acres of land. (Lib. 2, fol. 195, Jan. 16, 1667.) Records at Annapolis give the following memoranda of his offices: 1668—Lt. Ninian Beall. 1676—Lt. of Lord Baltimore's "Yacht of War, Loyal Charles of Maryland, John Goade Commander." 1684—Deputy Surveyor of Charles Co.; 1688—Appointed Chief Military Officer of Calvert Co.; 1689—Major of Calvert Co. Militia; 1692—High Sheriff of Calvert Co.; 1694—Colonel of Militia; 1697—On a Commission to treat with the Indians; 1679—1701, member of General Assembly; 1699—General Assembly passed an Act of Gratitude for the distinguished Indian services of Colonel Ninian Beall:

"Whereas Colonell Ninian Beall has been found very serviceable to this Province upon all incursions and disturbances of neighboring Indians and though now grown very aged and less able to perform well, continues—now beyond his ability to do the like service att this juncture of affairs, it is therefore thought fitt in point of gratitude for such his good

1 Mackenzie, C. N., Col. Fam. of the U. S., vol. II: 57.

services done and towards his support and relief now in his old age to make him an allowance out of public revenues of this province — Be it therefore enacted by the King's most excellent Majestie and by and with the advice and consent of this present General Assembly and the authority of the same, that Mr. William Hutchison, a member of this House as a trustee for and on behalf of the said Coll. Ninian Beall hath hereby given to him full power and authority to procure and purchase three good serviceable negro slaves for the proper use and benefit of him the said Coll. Ninian Beall - - -".

(Md. Arch. vol. XXII, fol. 494).

May 2, 1700, Col. Beall sent to Col. Addison bills of exchange amounting to 200 Pounds, which he had loaned "the Countrey to pay the rangers." (Md. Arch. XXIV, p. 55).

Before 1690, Col. Beall gave land in Upper Marlboro upon which a church (Presbyterian) was to be erected. For a minister, he turned to the Rev. Nathaniel Taylor, one of his 200 immigrants from Scotland. In 1707 Col. Beall presented the church with a costly silver communion service set. Today (1936) the church and the silver set are moved to Hyattsville, Md., and an Episcopal Church has risen on the old site at Upper Marlboro.

Col. Ninian Beall had 12 children, as follows:
1. John Beall, 1670-1711; 4 children
2. Capt. Charles Beall, b. 1672. Commissioned Lt. of Indian Rangers 1704.
3. Ninian, b. 1674; d. 1710. m. 1700 Elizabeth Magruder, dau. Col. Samuel Magruder.
4. Sarah, m. Col. Samuel Magruder.
5. Hester, m. 1707 Col. Joseph Belt.
6. Jane, m. Col. Archibald Edmonston.
7. Rachel.
8. Col. George Beall, b. 1695, d. 1780; m. Elizabeth Brooke, dau. Col. Thomas and Barbara Brooke.
9. Mary, m. Andrew Hambleton (South of Eastern Branch).
10. Thomas, d. 1708 unmarried.
11. Margery, m. (1st) Thomas Sprigg; (2) Col. Joseph Belt, her brother-in-law.
12. James.

One of Ninian Beall's granddaughters, Elizabeth, dau. of
Col. George Beall, b. 1743 and d. 1803, married Mr. Walter
Evans of the Eastern Branch.

Through his many acts of faithfulness and bravery, and
because of the large number of immigrants to his credit,
Ninian Beall was given warrants for thousands of acres of
land. His home, mentioned in his will (1717) was near
Upper Marlboro, Md. He died at Fifes Largo, named for the
place of his birth, in Scotland. As Deputy Surveyor, he seated
many families along the Eastern Branch and the Potomac in
Scotland Hundred, most of them through his own land warrants. Some of the patentees were as follows:

> Andrew Clarke, 1685, "Meurs", warrant unto
> Ninian Beall.
> Walter Thompson, 1685, "The Nock," warrant
> unto Ninian Beall.
> Benjamin Haddock, 1685, "Seaman's Delight,"
> war't. Nin. Beall.
> Walter Evans, 1698, "Nameless," warrant unto
> Ninian Beall.
> Thomas Ellis, 1685, "Mount Arraratt," war't.
> Ninian Beall.

"Inclosure," on the Eastern Branch, 1503 acres surveyed
for Ninian Beall and by him taken up in 1687, was a tract now
(1936) part of the National Aboretum. A portion of it extending south and west of the junction of Bladensburg Road
and the Boundary (now called Florida Avenue), was included
in the Federal City as laid out by General Washington and
Major L'Enfant, 1791. Col. Beall sold 1,047 acres of this tract,
in 1709, to his friend Major Richard Marsham, whose daughter
married Samuel Queen. (Rent Roll No. 3, fol. 352, Annap.)

On the eastern side of the Anacostia River the land belonged to Col. Beall above the land of the Addisons. "Fife
Enlarged," 1,050 acres, named for Fifeshire, Scotland, was
deeded by Col. Beall to his son Capt. Charles Beall, who died
in 1740.

In the western portion of the area later covered by the
National Capital, early taken up by various grants, there was
no opportunity for ownership by Col. Ninian Beall until the
end of the 17th Century. His interests had centered on the

area, however, probably through his early trips to the Garrison at the Falls. Possibly the route he took, down the steep banks of Rock Creek to the place of the shallow ford, followed the path made in earlier days by Indians and later traversed by the Rangers. Eventually, Col. Beall was successful in obtaining tracts on both sides of Rock Creek, "Rock of Dumbarton," 705 acres purchased from Henry Darnall and patented in 1703, and on the eastern side of Rock Creek, nearly opposite "Rock of Dumbarton," his earlier tract, "Beall's Levells," 225 acres between Mr. Hutchison's land and the tract called "Widow's Mite."

It is recorded that George Beall, son of Ninian's son Ninian, was born in 1729 in the home built on "Rock of Dumbarton."

Patent for "Beall's Levels," 225 Acres.
Recorded November the 4th, 1702.
Granted unto Col. Ninian Beall of Prince Georges County for five hundred and twenty acres dated the sixth day of May one thousand seven hundred and two I have surveyed and laid out for the said Beall all that tract of land lyeing in the said County called Bealls Levells Beginning at the South East bounded tree of a parcell of Land taken up by Mr. William Hutchison on the North Side of Goose Creeke and running thence North sixty perches to a parcell of land called the Widdowes mite, then East three hundred thirty seven perches, then South one hundred and fifty perches, then with a Straight line drawn to the first bounder Containing and now layed out for two hundred and twenty five acres of land to be held of the Mannor of Calverton.

per me Clement Hill, Junr. Surveyor
Gen'll. of the Western Shore.

18 November 1703—Then issued patt to ye above Beall of the above Land in p'suance of ye bond Cert Rent 9 Shillings Sterling.
(Pats., D.D. No. 5, fol. 81. Land Office, Annapolis, Md.)

ORIGINAL LAND OWNERS
IN THE DISTRICT OF COLUMBIA IN MARYLAND
PREVIOUS TO 1700

Tract owned	Name of Owner	Date	Annapolis Reference
Aaron 500 acres	William Hutchinson (Cert. in name of John Addison)	1688	Lib. 22, fol. 398 Pat. N. S. No. B, fol. 615
Analostien Island (Also called Barbadoes) 75 acres	Randolph Brandt	1682	Lib. 21, fol. 363 Pat. C. B. No. 3, fol. 48
Attwoods Purchase	John Attwood	1685	Lib. 22, fol. 165
	William Atcheson	1698 (cir.)	Pat. C. C. No. 4, fol. 144
Barbadoe 250 acres	Richard Evans	1685	Lib. 22, fol. 164 Pat. 1B & 1L No. C, fol. 192
Bealls Adventure 500 acres	Thomas Beall	1687	Lib. 22, fol. 266 Pat. N. S. No. 2, fol. 326
Berrys Purchase	William Berry		Unpatented certif. in Pr. Geo. Co.
Blewplayne 1,000 acres	George Thompson	1662 1663	Lib. 6, fol. 176
(The) Brothers Joint Interest 236 acres	Thomas Dent & Wm. Hatton		Lib. 13, fol. 10 Lib. 14, fol. 427
Brothers Purchase 780 acres	Zachariah Wade & Luke Gardner	1670	Lib. 19, fol. 570 Pat. C. C. No. 4, fol. 144
Carlyle 148 acres	John Addison and Willian Hutchinson	1695	Pat. B. B. No. 3, fol. 170-171
Chichester 400 acres	John Meekes	1664	Lib. 6, fol. 335-336

Original Land Owners in the District of Columbia in Maryland Previous to 1700

Tract owned	Name of Owner	Date	Annapolis Reference
Cuckolds Delight 200 acres	Thomas Green	1687	Lib. 22, fol. 240 Pat. 1B & 1L No. C, fol. 320
Dan 208 acres	Daniel Elliott	1695	Pat. B.B. No. 3, fol. 235-236
Duddington Manor 1,000 acres	George Thompson	1663	Lib. 6, fol. 174
Duddington Pasture 300 acres	George Thompson	1663	Lib. 6, fol. 174
Edloes Adventure 300 acres	Edward Edloe	1695	Pat. C No.3, fol. 559
Eglington 300 acres	James White	1670	Lib. 12, fol. 635 Lib. 14, fol. 117
Elkenhead 500 acres	William Taneyhill	1685	Lib. 22, fol. 165 Pat. N. S. No. B, fol. 145
Fathers Gift 500 acres	Richard and William Pinner	1666	Lib. 10, fol. 284 Lib. 11, fol. 351
(The) Forrest 712 acres	Henry Darnall	1695	Pat. C. No. 3, fol. 228
Fox Hall 150 acres	Ninian Beall Certif. to William Hutchison	1687	Lib. 22, fol. 272 Pat. N. S. No. 2, fol. 532
(The) Friendship	John Addison and William Hutchison	1695	Pat. C No. 3, fol. 100-101
(The) Gyrles Portion 1,776 acres	Henry Darnall (Chas. Co., now D. C.)	1688	Lib. 22, fol. 319 Pat. N. S. No. 2, fol. 724

Original Land Owners in the District of Columbia in Maryland Previous to 1700

Tract owned	Name of Owner	Date	Annapolis—Reference
(The) Grange 500 acres	Henry Jowles	1685	Lib. 22, fol. 166 Pat. N. S. No. 2, fol. 91
Greenes Purchase 200 acres	Joseph Harrison Certif. to Luke Green	1671	Lib. 11, fol. 438 Lib. 14, fol. 413
Guisborough 370 acres	George Thompson William Dent Possession Edmond Howard Rent Roll 8, fol. 314.	1663 1695	Pat. B. B. No. 3, fol. 207
Hadducks Hills 500 acres	Benjamin Hadduck	1685	Lib. 22, fol. 166 Pat. N. S. No. B, fol. 184
Houp Yard 500 acres	Walter Houp	1686	Lib. 22, fol. 240 Pat. IB & IL No. C fol. 276
Hudsons Range 500 acres	William Hudson	1685	Pat. 22, fol. 166
Inclosure 1,503 acres	Ninian Beall	1687	Lib. 22, fol. 323 Pat. N. S. No. 2, fol. 721
Jamaica 500 acres	John Pearce or Pierce	1687	Lib. 22, fol. 268 Pat. N. S. No. 2, fol. 310
Kendal Meadows 550 acres	William Digges	No date	Pat. T. I. No. 1, fol. 430, 59
Layton Stone	John Lewger	1666 (cir.)	Lib. 10, fol. 284 Lib. 11, fol. 351
Little Deane 103 acres	Thomas James	1696	Pat. B. B. No. 3, fol. 166

Original Land Owners in the District of Columbia in Maryland Previous to 1700

Tract owned	Name of Owner	Date	Annapolis—Reference
Maidens Delight 65 acres	Henry Givin	1686	Lib. 22, fol. 213 Pat. N. S. No. B fol. 368
500 acres Meurs	Andrew Clarke	1685	Lib. 22, fol. 268 Pat. N. S. No. 2, fol. 353
Mount Araratt 150 acres	Thomas Ellis	1685	Pt. C. C. No. 4, fol. 72-73
Nameless 230 acres	Walter Evans	1698	Pat. C. C. No. 4, fol. 144
New Bottle	John Watson	1687	Lib. 22, fol. 267 Pat. I. B. & I. L. No. C, fol. 309
(The) New Designe 281 acres	Ignatius Wheeler		Pat. C. C. No. 4, fol. /1
New Troy 500 acres	George Thompson	1663	Lib. 6, fol. 174
(The) Nock 500 acres	Walter Thompson	1686	Lib. 22, fol. 214 Pat. N. S. No. B, fol. 372
Padworth Farme 600 acres	George Yates	1681	Lib. 21, fol. 175 Pat. C. B. No. 2, fol. 465
Pencotts Invention 239 acres	James Pencott	1687	Lib. 22, fol. 306 N. S. No. 2 fol. 465
Port Royall 500 acres	John Pearce or Pierce	1685	Lib. 22, fol. 276 Pat. N. S. No. 2, fol. 310, 330
(The) Prospect 52 acres	Thomas Brooke	1695	Pat. C. No.3, fol. 263

Original Land Owners in the District of Columbia in Maryland Previous to 1700

Tract owned	Name of Owner	Date	Annapolis Reference
Red Bud Thickett 113 acres	Ignatius Wheeler	1698	Pat. C. C. No. 4, fol. 60
Rome 400 acres	Francis Pope	1663	Lib. 6, fol. 318, 319
Saint Elizabeth 1,430 acres	George Thompson John Addison (To Notley Rozier through his wife Jane Digges)	1663 1669	Pat. G. C. No.4, fol. 95 Pat. W. D. fol. 147
Saint Phillip and Jacob 400 acres	Phillip Lines	1675	Lib. 15, fol. 264 Lib. 19, fol. 83
Salcom 300 acres	John Evans	1687	Lib. 22, fol. 267 Pat. I. B. & I. L. No. C, fol. 308
Salom (or Salop?) 300 acres	Robert Mason	1687	Lib. 22, fol. 267
Scotland 300 acres	William Thompson	1685	Lib. 22, fol. 164 Pat. N. S. No. B, fol. 148
Scotland Yard 500 acres	Robert Troope	1664	Lib. 6, fol. 333-334.
Seamans Delight 500 acres	Benjamin Hadduck	1685	Lib. 22, fol. 167 Pat. N. S. No. 2, fol. 92
Ship Landing 21 acres	William Murdock		Pat. B. C. & G. S. No. 5, fol. 172 Pat. B. C. & G. S. No. 2, fol. 398
Strabane 500 acres	John Scott	1685	Lib. 22, fol. 211 Pat. N. S. No. 2, fol. 181

Original Land Owners in the District of Columbia in Maryland Previous to 1700

Tract owned	Name of Owner	Date	Annapolis Reference
Three Sisters	Thomas Hillary	1684	Lib. 22, fol. 20 Pat. N. S. No. 4, fol. 14
Virginia Garden 185 acres	Frances Presley	1695	Pat. B. B. No. 3, fol. 255-256
White Haven 759 acres	John Addison and William Hutchison	1695	Pat. B. B. No. 3, fol. 164
Whitelaintine 300 acres	Christopher Thompson	1685	Pat. N. S. No. B, fol. 140
Widows Mite 600 acres	John Langworth	1666	Lib. 10, fol. 528 Pat. I. B. & I. L. No. C, fol. 166
Yarrow 500 acres	James Thompson	1677	Lib. 22, fol. 268 Pat. N. S. No. 2, fol. 301
Yarrowhead 506 acres	James Stoddard	1695	Pat. B. B. No. 3, fol. 194

ORIGINAL LAND OWNERS
IN THE DISTRICT OF COLUMBIA IN VIRGINIA

One must be on the Maryland side of the Potomac to appreciate the gorgeous sunsets back of the wooded hills of Virginia. The brilliance seems to rise as a halo to mark the land which gave birth to that gentleman from Mount Vernon whose desires and dreams brought about the capital city at Washington. One must be on the Virginia side of the Potomac, however, to view the results of General Washington's endeavors. The two viewpoints, each centered on the Nation's Capital, are bound forever by the majestic Potomac. Termination of the original part of the District of Columbia in Virginia, less than a hundred years ago, was no barrier to the union that today, in 1936, has grown more binding than ever.

Before 1700, the Rangers in Virginia and the Rangers in upper Maryland had found a crossing accessible at the lower Falls. This, too, had probably been used from "time immemorial" by the Indians native to these areas. The Virginia shore, beginning west of Analostan (now Theodore Roosevelt) Island to the mouth of Great Hunting Creek, below Alexandria, was granted by patent of Sir William Berkeley to Robert Howsing, a Welch ship captain trading in Virginia, in October, 1669. Previous to that time, land speculators had ventured into the territory and had obtained patents from the Northern Neck proprietors. At the time, however, the Virginia side of the Potomac opposite the future site of Washington was a settlement of Anacostian Indians who held the place to themselves successfully, and prevented occupation by the white man until near the end of that century.

(One of these adventurers was John Custis of the Eastern Shore, founder of the Custis family in Virginia. In 1657 he obtained a patent for 2,000 acres "above Annacosties," for transporting 40 immigrants to Virginia.)

The "Howsing Patent," 6,000 acres, within the year it was made was assigned by Howsing to John Alexander for six hogsheads of tobacco. Alexander, who lived down the Potomac in what is now King George County, was the immigrant ancestor of the family of that name, for whom Alexandria, Va., formerly called "Belhaven," was renamed. It is

The Howsing-Alexander Tract, Virginia
Surveys of 1698-1741

to a descendant of Charles Alexander of that family, Mrs.
C. A. S. Sinclair, that we are indebted for a copy of the ancient
survey made in 1741. The survey was based upon the original
survey of 1693, of which no copies now exist.

The survey of 1693 was made by Theodorick Bland,[1]
surveyor of Stafford County (then the northern county of
Virginia). The map of 1741, made by Joseph Berry for Messrs.
John and Gerrard Alexander, antedates the early map of "Belhaven" made by George Washington before Alexandria as a
town was begun.

Pearsons Island, shown on the Joseph Berry map, south
of "Four-Mile Creek," was settled by Alexander Pearson in
1695.[2] Analostan Island (now Theodore Roosevelt Island), is
also shown on the map, inscribed with the name "My
Lord's Island." Directly west of Analostan Island, on
the shore and at the end of the Howsing-Alexander tract,
"Richard Wheeler's Plantation" is recorded,. At the other
end of the tract, the mouth of Great Hunting Creek, where
now is "Jones Point," was then "Pipers Island" and "Mr. Phil-
lip Alexander's Land."

In the late eighteenth and early nineteenth centuries, des-
cendants of John Alexander established homes near the mouth
of Four Mile Run (then called Four-Mile Creek), and named
these places "Preston," "Mount Ida," and "Summer Hill."
The wife of Mr. Charles Alexander of "Preston" was a great
(3rd)-grandmother of Mrs. C. A. S. Sinclair of today and a
great (3rd)-aunt of your writer.

John Parke Custis built his "Abington" on this land, fac-
ing the Potomac River. Later his son, George Washington
Parke Custis, built his "Arlington" on the lovely wooded hill
so beloved by the people of Washington today.

A list of the earliest patentees of this region, whose patents faded into the distance before the Howsing grant, was
compiled by Fairfax Harrison in his "Landmarks of Old
Prince William." Mr. Harrison states that the patents of these
men, naming no county, are not included in the county index
in the Land Office of Virginia. As Mr. Harrison's "Landmarks
of Old Prince William" is exhausted and the copies are no
longer available, I take the liberty of repeating here his list
of the earliest patentees. The reference he gives is as follows:

Patents, 4: 156, 170, 171, 172, 174, 177, 228, 229, 258, 259, 281, 305, 307, 309, 363, 571.

James Ashton	John Ayres	John Bennett
George Berry	Thomas Boswell	Robert Bradshaw
Thomas Broughton	William Butler	Francis Carpenter
Francis Clay	Robert Clerke	John Cloughton
Vincent Cock	John Custis	William Davis
Francis Gray	John Hayles	William Knott
John Launcelot	Hugh Lee	William Presley
Henry Randolph	John Raven	John Tingy
Edward Williams	John Wood	Thomas Woodhouse

1 and
2 Chas W. Stetson. "Washington's Woods on Four Mile Run." Col. Hist. Soc. vol. 35-36, 1935.

ORIGINAL OWNERSHIP OF
ANALOSTAN ISLAND

(Now called Theodore Roosevelt Island)

The earliest record of this island is in the patent to Robert Howsing, October 21, 1669, for 6,000 acres of land along the Potomac River to a point "neare opposite to a small island commonly called and known by the name "My Lord's Island."

The map of Augustine Herrman, published in 1673, designates the island as "Anacostien Ile." This map was made several years prior to its publication, however, and may have antedated the Howsing patent.

In 1680, a special warrant for land was given by Lord Baltimore to Captain Randolph Brandt of Charles County, Maryland, for his service in protecting the colonists from Indians. In 1682, the island was granted to Brandt. A copy of the document is here given.

"To the Right Hon'ble, the Lord Propri'y:
In obedience to a special warrant from his Lordship bearing date the 21st of July, 1680, granted unto Capt. Randolph Brandt of Charles County upon a petition—These are in humble manner to certify that I Richard Edelen Depty Sur. for St. Maries County under the Honorable Vincent Lowe, Esq., Sur. Gen'l. of this Province, and in reference to a warrant granted the said Brandt bearing date the 27th of

April last past, for two hundred acres, have laid out for the said Brandt one certain parcel of land being the Island lying in Potomack River near the falls of said river over against Rock Creek in Charles County commonly called or known by the name of the Analostian Island, containing by estimation seventy-five acres more or less—To behold of Zachiah Manor called Barbadoes—Certified this twenty-ninth day of April, Anno Dom. 1682.

                                        Richard Edelin."

Randolph Brandt, Cert., 75 acres; Patent A. C. No, 3.48; Rent 3½ Pounds. **Barbadoes.**

                        (Records at Annapolis, Md.)

In the will of Randolph Brandt of Charles County, Md., dated December 29, 1697, and probated February 10, 1698 (Md. Cal. Wills No. 2), the "island Barbadoes, near falls of Potomac River, 75 acres," is left to his daughter Margaret, wife of Francis Hammersley, and their heirs.

Francis Hammersly, on August 28th, 1717, transferred all rights to the island to George Mason,[1] from whom it descended to General John Mason, whose home on the island, is today (1936) only visible among the ruins.

----

1 U. S. vs.: M. F. Morris et al. Record 7, vol. 5, p. 2127-2128.

PART THREE
IN THE TIME OF THE INDIANS

To nature lovers, signs of spring in the woods of the District of Columbia and along the shores of the upper Potomac bring promise of delights in store, pine-scented forests and wild flowers. In days of old, however, with all the loveliness of spring there came the worry of lurking Indians, for this was the time hunters went forth to replenish food supplies depleted during winter.

Nature's delightful endowments at Tohoga, pictured so aptly by Henry Fleet, probably were the cause of the many Indian settlements about the area now called the District of Columbia. The location of these settlements is clearly defined on maps and records in the Bureau of Ethnology, Smithsonian Institution. Some of them were along the east banks of the Anacostia River, or Eastern Branch; others on the Virginia shore almost opposite Analostan (now Theodore Roosevelt)

Island. Along the banks of Piney Branch, near Pierce Mill, and westward over Ridge Road, on the Loughboro Estate, and to the Potomac, remains have been found of settlements of Indians.[1]

In addition to these modern discoveries, however, the searcher of ancient records finds wierd tales of the actual, everyday lives of these Indians and their relations with the colonists.

---

1 Hand book of American Indians, vol. I.

Esquire Tom

Deep in the Archives of Maryland is hidden the story of Esquire Tom, a character dreaded in Maryland as well as in Virginia. The setting begins about sixty years before Esquire Tom comes into the story in his limelight of fear and terror. Incidentally, he brought about the first standing army and the first Government fort in the area later to become the District of Columbia.

After the first negotiations[1] in 1635, between the Colonists and the Indians, relations between the two in the lower parts of Maryland were peaceful. In 1666, the Maryland government cemented its friendly relations by making a formal treaty with the Piscataways, and in 1668 certain of Lord Baltimore's tracts, or manors, were set up to accomodate and protect the tribesmen from the fierce hunting Indians of the north.[2] One of these tracts, it is believed, was near the mouth of Rock Creek;[3] another was on the Maryland side of the Potomac opposite the site of Mount Vernon.[4]

After the treaty with the Piscataways, both the English and the Indians of the Potomac fought off the dreaded Susquehannas, a tribe of warlike barbarians whose men were "seven foot high—their voices large and hollow as ascending out of a Cave, their gate stately and majestic."[5] These were Indians

---

1 Father Andrew White's "Journals": 30 miles of land at St. Marys purchased from the Indians for axes, hatchets, rakes, and several yards of cloth.
2 Md. Arch. vol. V, p. 165.
3 Fairfax Harrison, Landmarks of Old. Pr. Wm. vol.I. p. 94.
4 Fairfax Harrison, Landmarks of Old Pr. Wm. vol.I. p. 94.
5 Fairfax Harrisson, Landmarks of Old Pr. Wm. vol. I. p. 94.

of the Northern Tribes, others of whom immediately sided
against the Piscataways. They included the Senecas, above
Great Falls of the Potomac, and the Iroquois in Virginia who
had come from the North by way of the Blue Ridge. The Iroquois path along the mountains is shown on the Fry and Jef-
ferson map of 1751, and is referred to in Joshua Fry's description, as "the Indian road which had been in their possession since the year 1684."

These tribes sought to separate the Piscataways from the
colonists, and in many ways resorted to cunning. Their schem-
ing was so persistent and yet so unapparent that the younger
men of the Piscataways eventually were completely won over,
and at the invitation of the mountain tribes, moved themselves
across the Potomac and into the hills of Virginia.[6]

The danger of this move was foreseen by the Maryland
Assembly. It implied a subjection to the Five Nations and
future trouble for the Colonists. They therefore ordered:

That a commission be sent to the Piscataways in the
mountains to learn from them why they deserted their habi-
tations in Maryland, and to make proposals to them for their
return. Mr. William Hutchison, owner of a Maryland tract at
Rock Creek, a tract on the Potomac just below the Eastern
Branch, and one at Mattawoman Creek, was sent to Virginia
with the appointed commission. On returning, the commission
reported to the Assembly (in part):

> "The Indians answered that the occasion of their
> fflight so suddenly and in that manner was to secure
> their wives and children; for they understood that
> the English fforces were ordered to come down upon
> them in a few days—and they did not think them-
> selves secure till fforted in that place. They seemed
> well pleased [with our proposal] and cheerfully an-
> swered that they would return as soon as possibly
> they could go into the Governm't of Maryland and set-
> tle either at their old ffort nigh Piscattoway or about
> Rock Creek;—but they could not remove their
> families till the next spring, Corn being planted and
> wed there, and fflourishing; the women and children
> not able to travell, etc."

Mr. Hutchison being called in by his Excellency is told
that he having lived near the Piscattoway ffort (Maryland)

---

for some years and had communication with them, asks him his sentiments of the said Indians, whether he believes they will come back or no; who says that it is his belief they will scarce come back, by reason the Virginians (as he is informed) infused strange notions in their heads by telling them that if they go back to Maryland they will be destroyed, and that so long as they keep in Virginia they will be safe.

Next a letter from Major William Dent, at Nanjemy, was read. He said:

> "I am this day advised that the Indians in Virginia are preparing a very great present for the Govr. of Virginia, Vizt: Every man must give a Beaver Skin, and those that have none, as much Roanoke as will purchase one, and this tax is layd on all the Indians in these upper parts, and my author says in the lower parts also, but that seems to me something improbable.—My author is my Brother Gerrard ffowke, and he had it from a Piscattaway Indian. I have not seen my Brother Mason, but expect him every day."
> (Md. Arch. 24: 325, Nov. 31, 1697).

Nevertheless, at this Assembly, October 14, 1697, "several accounts were produced and read concerning the late assassination committed by Indians on the body of one William Wiggenton's wife and three children in Stafford County, Virginia, —how a certain Indian called Esquire Tom, one of the chief actors of the afore-mentioned villany had made his escape from thence into these parts in Maryland, and it being signified by another paper read that the said Indian Esquire Tom has since been seen and spoke with by some English inhabitants of Charles County, and suffered to escape notwithstanding his Excellency's proclamation for the seizing and apprehending."

One of the accounts: "Deposition of Capt. Ebenezar Blakiston of Coecill County, Md., aged fforty Seaven years or thereabouts. This Depnt. Saith.—That being at Coll. ffitzhughs House in Stafford County in his Majestie's Colony of Virga. on or about the 8th of this Instant July, he heard it reported that there were about 10 Indians at Capt. Brents House which had got in drink and were troublesome, inso much that he commended their Arms to be delivered up; ffive whereof warned accordingly, but three more that had also Arms would not part with them, but made their escape; that the next day the sd. Indians marcht to a house about two miles below the said Capt. Brents where they assaulted and wounded a man's wife and ffour small children in dangerous manner. That this Depont. went himself from Coll. ffitzhugh's to the sd. house (being about 10 miles distant) for to know the Certainty; where he see the Woman and discoursed with her, who informed him that as she was washing of butter at the Spring, there came two Indians up to her and she Striving to get over a ffence to make her Escape, they knockt her down, but she was not sensible what they did to her afterwards. That when she came to herself she felt her Breast very Sore and her Scalp all taken off except a little hair left on her forhead. That he discoursed Doctor Tanckardson, who has her under Care, who peneth that her right Breast has been Ript up by the Indians with a Knife insomuch that when he came to dress it, the wind pusht out like a pair of Bellowes. That the Woman's oldest daughter lyes dangerously wounded, and is thought will not live. That the neighbors have got three of her children which they report are also wounded, but not mortally."

A letter was read from Mr. John Addison to Capt. Richard Brightwell, Commander of the Rangers upon Potomack, dated July 13, 1697: (Md. Arch., vol. 23, p. 175.)

"This evening came John the Frenchman from Virginia and saith that John Peeke, one of Capt. Mason's troop, came up this evening and gave Acct. that a woman and three children at the head of Acquio Creek was on Sunday morning last murdered by Indians; I send you this notice that you may keep the stricter eye abroad."

A letter dated July 22, 1697, from Capt. George Mason to Coll. Addison was read: "On the 8th instant the Indians did att. the house of Wm. Wigentons on Ocquio in the heart of our County and Kill as they thought a woman and three children; they did mortally wound them. The woman's head was clean slead, and Stab'd in the side with a great knife, but Thank God all of them are alive and like to Recover. * * On Tuesday, the 27th, they ordered all our Justices and militia officers to meet me at our Ct. House. I have sent for the Emperor and his great men to be there. Capt. Brightwell's

information I never heard off, but our County is so Dam'd
full of lyes; that I know not how allmost to act, but God
direct for the best that I may act both for Good of King and
Countrey."

A letter from Capt. Geo. Brent, [of Virginia] June 29,
1697, to the Governor [of Maryland] explained the whole situ-
ation. Said Mr. Brent, "One main thing was wanting (to wit)
upon what grounds these disorders have been committed, and
since writing the above, vizt., this evening, it hath been my
good fortune to make some discovery in that point.

"This evening, I called at our High Sherriffs
where Choptico Robin (one of the band)——told me
he would now (being set free) make me fully sensible
of the cause of this villany——. Early in the spring,
to wit, about five months last passed, Esquire Tom
was at or about the Falls of Potomock, and there were
some Piscattoway Indians and some of those Seniquos
that live in the mountains, amongst which last was a
Susquehanna, a Great Man whose name is Monges.
This Indian had much private communication with
Esquire Tom.——He p'sented him with a large belt
of Peak, and told him that his Nation was Ruin'd
by the English assisted by Piscattays and now they
were no People; that he had still tears in his eyes
when he thought of it, and not being able to do any-
thing in Publique he must take his revenge in private by his money, and therefore if this Esq. Tom
would kill some English where he could with great-
est safety do it and most probably be laid upon the
Emperor's people, he would give him[Esquire Tom]
great rewards. —— The English would first bleed
and then revenge it upon his Indian enemies. Esquire Tom promised to do this. The thing was proposed to be committed in Maryland, but [recently]
since the man had been killed there, both the Emperor and Pamunky Indians had fled to Virginia, so
this Robin the Relator (Chaptico Robin) with Esq.
Tom and one Indian more, Rann back from their
company and Esq Tom and the other Indians did the
mischief, and this Robin kept Sentry that all the rest
of the company knew of the thing only "the Deaf
Indian"—

So pardon the prolixity that Necessity Drawes
Naratives under, and Accept the Zeal of
                    Your Most Humble Servant,
                              George Brent.

There followed in October, a "general proclamation issued to the several counties of the Province by His Excellency ffr. Nicholson at Nanjemy in Charles County this 28th Day of July in the 9th Year of His Majestie's Reign,1697; this for the seizing and apprehending of the said Esquire Tom, and that a reward of 10 pounds Sterll. be therein ascertained to the party or parties that shall take and deliver him up in Virginia aforesaid."[1]

The Standing Army

October 15, 1697. The Council[2] again Sate and were Present.

His Excellency is pleased to propose: That for the security of the planters of this Province against invasion of Indians or the like, there be chosen out of the Six Counties of the Western Shore 200 men such as can be spared in order to be allwaies in readinesss upon any warning of Rendezvous, where all necessary Arms, etc., are to be lodged ready to fit and equip them up for service; and that each person appointed find himself a good horse and that the Publick and Armes be well fitted for that purpose.——That they recommend some Fitt Persons for Officers to command those men who shall receive commissions accordingly, that none of these men be taken out of the frontier plantations.——

The Navy

That there be two or three Boats provided and got ready to be kept in the most convenient places upon Potomock, for sending expresses or the like (upon any Occasion) by water.

The Earliest Ferry

October 16, 1697.

This Committee do think it necessary that there be one good and substantial boat provided to be kept towards the head of Potomock by some careful person as His Excellency shall think fitt, such a one as will carry a couple of horses over the River and may be rowed and Sayled, and do desire that His Excellency will give orders for the same.

---

1 Esquire Tom eventually was captured by enemy Indians, who spirited him away.
2 Referring, of course, to the Maryland Council.

The Wild Horses

Ordered by the Assembly: That the Rangers belonging
to the Garrison of Potomock and Baltimore be permitted to
take up one or two wild, unmarked horses apiece (being
deemed for his Majestie's Service) provided they break and
train them up for the use of their Ranging, and not sell them.

The Rangers

Produced and read an act to appoint Rangers for the defence of this Province, wherein is a clause empowering his
Excellency the Governor to levy the sum of 60,000 pounds of
tobacco upon occasion during intervals of Assembly. It was
agreed and thought convenient that the said sum should be
now levied.

Recommended: that the Hon. Coll. Jno. Addison, who
lives convenient to the head of the Potomack and has been
already very serviceable in those parts, be appointed and have
power to go and visit the Garrison and said men once a fort
night, for which he may be satisfied out of the publick.

Likewise, that the said Governor of Virginia be desired
to give orders to the Rangers upon the frontiers for to settle
themselves somewhere near the falls for the better inter-
course to be had betwixt them and the Maryland Rangers
for the mutual defence of each Government.

That if the said men can not find themselves with necessary provisions, so that they need not quit their posts in look-
ing after it; it is proposed to Coll. Addison whether he will
furnish them, to be allowed for the same out of the Publick.
To which he says he is willing to undertake, as also the other
proposition for visiting the Garrison.

Ordered, that no person upon any prejudice whatsoever
do presume to sell any Syder or other strong liquor to any
of the men at the Garrison or to other persons appointed to
range at the Eastern Branch without the special leave of the
Hon. Coll. John Addison.

Coll. Addison and Mr. Hutchins., owners of the land where
the Garrison is kept, being asked whether the Rangers may
have leave to plant Corn in any of those Indian fields and
clear the hill there near the ffort. Do make answer that they
may freely do the same without any disturbance.

The New Fort

Ordered, that a ffort be built upon the top of sd. Hill near the other ffort, and that the said Hill be cleared by the Souldiers at the Garrison, and that the Hon. Coll. Jno. Addison take care to get a house built there, at the cheapest rate he can; but that he do not actually build the same until he see whether the Indians return thither or not; yet however, that he gett the timber ready for the Stockadoes and see that the hill be cleared; and that he purchase a couple of small Gunns (which are in the possession of Capt. George Harris) at the cheapest rate he can, also provide two or three good Canooes, beside a good substantial boat, reported by the Committee to be necessary to be Gott; for all which he is to be paid out of the Pub. leavy of this Province.

Ordered: that the 13 men and two officers this day agreed upon to be raised for the strengthening the Garrison and frontiers upon Potomack be forthwith raised accordingly and sent up to be appointed their stations by the Hon. Coll. Jno. Addison of Prince Georges County; the which said men are to be raised as follows, vizt: Four out of Annarrundell County; three out of Calvert; three out of Saint Maries; and three out of Charles County. And that Richard Owen of Ann arrundell county be Captain to command part of the said men, and Giles Hill of Saint Maries County Lt. to command another part thereof. Hereby directing and ordering that the Colonels of the said counties take care to Gett the said men raised with all imaginable expedition, to be impressed for the said service with their horses.

October 19, 1697.

Ordered: That the Honorable Coll. John Addison discourse Coll. Ninian Beal whether or not he be willing to continue in the commission he already has for raising men upon any disturbance of Indians.—The thirteen men and two officers for strengthening the Garrison and Frontiers of Potomack to be allwaies compleat that number.

The Government Interpreter

October 20, 1697.

Ordered: That Henry Moore of Charles County be constituted and impowered to be Gener'l Interpreter for this

Government upon any Treaty to be made with the Indians on
the Western Shore, and that no other p'son presume to take
upon him that office besides; hereby impowered, the Honbl.
Coll. Jno. Courts to administer an oath to the sd. Moore, faith-
fully to discharge his duty therein, whensoever he is by any
authority thereunto called or required.

The Anacostin Fort Today

The location today of this old fort may be found through
tracing the bounds of a survey and sale dated December 21,
1793, between Wm. Berry Warman of Prince Georges County
and James Greenleaf, of New York. (Lib. A, No.1, pt. 2, fol.
72, Land Records, Dist. of Col.) The fort is mentioned in the
sale of "Bayley's Purchase," the tract for which Mr. Greenleaf paid 5,750 pounds current money of Maryland. (Anacostin
Cove probably was St. Thomas Bay, which later became filled-
in land at the Washington Navy Yard.)

"Resurvey of Eltenhead, Fergusons Gain, Hamiltons Venture, Attwoods Purchase, and Berrys Purchase."

"Beginning for Bayley's Purchase at a stone
heretofore fixed in the place where was proved the
beginning tree of Atwoods Purchase formerly stood,
which said tree was the beginning of Greens Purchase and the beginning of another tract called
Aaron, the said stone is fixed on a point on the East
side of the Eastern Branch of Potomack River, a
little above the place where formerly stood the Anacostin Fort, and opposite to a bay or cove called the
Anacostin Cove, and from the said stone running with
the first line of Atwoods Purchase corrected, viz;
south 84 degrees 3 minutes, easterly 351½ perches,
to a bounded chestnut oak, being the beginning tree
of Hamilton's Venture and said to be the second
boundary of the tract called Aaron, then with the second land of Aaron corrected, viz.; south 71 degrees
30 minutes, easterly 189 perches to the place heretofore approved where stood a bounded white oak on
a Ridge, the 3rd line boundary of Aaron, which is in
a field near the south side of the Main Road leading
from the Eastern Branch Ferry towards Upper Marlborough, then with part of the 3rd line of Aaron corrected by an allowance of 2 degrees 30 minutes for

variation, viz; south 65 degrees, west 60 perches,
where it intersects with the main line of Hamilton's
Venture, etc. * * *
Containing 1,212 acres of land more or less, together with all houses, improvements, etc."

The Indians After 1700

One day in September, 1704, Ninian Beall made record
of the presence of Indians at that time lurking about the
Eastern Branch, or Anacostia.

Sept. 9, 1704.

"May it please your Excellency. I have been do-
ing my duty to render your Excellency an account
of the late murther that has been committed by the
Heathen in Virgina at Potowmack Creek. The last
of October, murthered one man, two women, one
child, and on Thursday last there came one Indian
from the mountains to the Eastern Branch, there being a great many Indians hunting in those places,
and hallowed over the Eastern Branch to some other
Indians at **Andrew Hamiltons,** they having a Cabbin
there, and the Indian went over to see what he hol-
lowed for and stayed with him all half an hour and
returned, and told the said Hambleton that they must
all go to the mountains tomorrow, being which they
are all in general gone. May it please your Excellency,
ammunition is very scarce in these parts. No more,
but your Excellency's humble servant to command
whilst

I am

Ninian Beale

These from Rock Creek

"Advised that his Excellency the Governor will
write to Coll. Beale to desire his utmost care and dili-
gence to prevent any mischief or disturbance in these
parts, and if any should happen to give his Excellency
and Coll. Addison the Speediest notice, and that if
any arms or ammunition are wanting thereupon care
will be taken to send what is requested and that he
apply to Coll. Addison for any ammunition."

(Md. Arch., vol. XXIV. Proc. of Assembly.)

Perhaps Col. Beall had come from his "Rock of Dumbarton" on Rock Creek, and had travelled by an Indian path
across the stretch of wooded land where the National Capital

in future years was to rise. The route was familiar to him
through the trips of his Rangers to the Garrison at the Falls.
And up the river beyond the Great Falls, he knew of the
route north and west to the Indian village Canavest. It was
from this village (beyond Sugarloaf Mountain) that the
Indians eventually journeyed to Ohio, and finally disappeared.

Early Roads at Washington, Before 1700

The early map-makers were heroes whose names
should be sung in any history of any mapped region. To their
ingenuity are we indebted, especially for the opening of public
highways. It was not until 1669 that the Maryland Assembly
made a law regarding the creation of highways for the
Province, and the making of heads of rivers, creeks, branches
and swamps passable for "Horse and ffoote." The law em-
powered commissioners for each county to mark out the most
convenient highways and paths, to appoint overseers, to levy
tobacco or labor-taxes, and to carry on the work, "Provided
that this Act shall not be to the apparent damage of any
p'ticular p'son by making or marking any high waye or path
through his Yard, Garden, Orchard, or Cornfield." (Md. Arch.,
vol. 2, May 27, 1669).

The Garrison maintained at the lower falls of the Potomac
for protection against Indians was a direct cause of the first
route across the area that later became the Nation's Capital.
On October 19, 1697, the Assembly issued an order "That
the Roads on each side of Eastern Branch of Potomack be
well cleared from plantation to plantation, and from the said
plantations to the Garrison." Along this route from the Eastern Branch to the Garrison went Ninian Beall many times, in
his supervision of the Potomac Rangers. At Rock Creek the
route led down its steep, rocky banks, and thence through
the shortest way to the falls (at Chain Bridge). After 1700,
Ninian Beall owned land on both sides of Rock Creek at this
point, Beall's Levels on the eastern shore, and Rock of Dumbarton on the west.

In 1699, the Maryland Assembly passed an Act (Md.
Arch., vol. 22, p. 475) as follows:

June-July, 1699.

An Act for making highways and making the heads of rivers, creeks, branches, and swamps passable for horse and foot." "All Publick and main roads to be hereafter cleared and well grubbed, fitt for travelling 20 foot wide and good and substantial bridges made over all heads of rivers, creeks, branches, and swamps where need shall require at the discretion of the justices of the county courts and for the better ascertaining what is or shall be deemed to be roads—be it likewise enacted that the justices of the county courts shall set down and ascertain in their records once every year what are the public roads of their respective counties and appoint overseers of the same, and that no person whatsoever shall alter or change any said public roads without the leave or licence of the Governor and Council or Justices of the county courts upon penalty of 500 lbs. of tobacco etc.—and that all the roads that lead to any ferrys, court house or to any church or leading through any county to the port of Annapolis shall be marked on both sides the road with two notches etc."

(Md. Arch., vol. 22, p. 475).

In 1737, a map was completed by Robert Brooke (of Essex County, Va.) showing the area along the Potomac from the Shenandoah Mountains down to Chapawamsic. The expenses of his map-making journey were paid by Virginia, to whom he presented the following bill:

"Dr:
Commissioners for His Majestie and the Right Honorable Thomas Lord Fairfax, for Sundry Expenses in Surveying Potomack River from ye Mo. of Shenendo to Chapawamsick—
1737.

To paid John Wilcoxen for ye use of his Canoe from Capt. Awbreys to Shenendo and down to Sinigar	10. 8.
To paid Capt. Awbrey for Liquors and provisions	5. 0.10.
To paid Mr. Bell for his son and Horse to bring our Things from Sinegar to Magees	1. 2.11.
To paid McGee for Victuals and Drink	7. 6.
To paid a Sloop man for 2 gals. of rum	8. 0.
To Mrs. Morton for Bread and Bacon	7.10.

Allowed—   RO: Brooke.—

Calendar of Virginia State Papers, 1652-1781. Vol. I, p. 229.

A Letter from Captain Richard Brightwell

Today, as we sweep about the streets of the Capital in
modern automobiles and within a few minutes can cross the
Potomac and be in Alexandria, it is interesting to think of
the lonely foot soldiers, the "Rangers upon Potomock," who
marked off on trees the early routes through the primeval
forests. I give you a report from their captain.

"October 12, 1697.

"Pursuant to your Excellency's command for returning an account of our ranging. I do humbly certify that according to your Excellency's order for
ranging in the frontiers, I have kept my men ranging
ever since to the Frontier plantations and up and
down the Eastern Branch towards the head of Patuxent to the frontiers there, and so back again, but have
not mett with any Indians in all our range, nor any-
thing worth noticing. And as to our Out Range, before the said order we kept constantly ranging from
our Garrison to the Sugar Lands, which we compute
to be about 40 miles, being generally stoney, rocky
land near the River, all the way thither, and barren
backwards; but the Sugar lands extraordinarily rich
and continue so for several miles backwards. From
the Sugar lands we ranged away towards the eastward to Potapsco which we compute to be about 50
miles, and so from thence make straight away to
the Garrison, which we compute to be betwixt 60
and 70 miles, in which range is generally good lands;
but we have not mett nor seen any Indians this twelve
months, except two back Indians that came to the
ffort here before Mr. Stodart's Negro boye was
Murthered, who came Civily into the ffort and were
suffered to depart without any disturbance.

"As for making any other discoveries, I know
of none to give an Accot. of; all which is humbly
certified this 12th day of October, Anno. 1697. By
your Excellency's

"Obedient and Faithful Humble Servant,

"RICHARD BRIGHTWELL"

PART FOUR

Some Old Documents

Excerpts from

"Narrative of A Voyage to Maryland"

By Father Andrew White

(Published in Scharf's History of Maryland, vol. I, and in Old South Leaflets, vol. VII.)

"Having now arrived at the wished-for-country, we allotted names according to circumstances. And indeed the Promontory, which is toward the south, we consecrated with the name of St. Gregory (now Smith Point), naming the northern one (now Point Lookout) St. Michael's, in honor of all the angels. Never have I beheld a larger or more beautiful river. The Thames seems a mere rivulet in comparison with it; it is not disfigured with any swamps, but has firm land on each side. Fine groves of trees appear, not choked with briers or bushes and undergrowth, but growing at intervals as if planted by the hand of man so that you can drive a four-horse carriage, wherever you choose, through the midst of the trees. Just at the mouth of the river we observed the natives in arms. That night, fires blazed through the whole country, and since they had never seen such a large ship, messengers were sent in all directions, who reported that a **Canoe**, like an island, had come with as many men as there were trees in the woods. We went on, however to Herons' Island, so called from the immense number of these birds. The first island we came to (we called it) St. Clement's Island, and, as it has a sloping shore, there is no way of getting to it except by wading. Here the women, who had left the ship, to do the washing, upset the boat, and came near being drowned, losing also a large part of my linen clothes, no small loss in these parts. . .

On the day of the Annunciation of the Most Holy Virgin Mary in the year 1634 we celebrated the mass for the first time on this island. This had never been done before in this part of the world. After we had completed the sacrifice, we took upon our shoulders a great cross, which we had hewn out of a tree, and advancing in order to the appointed place, with the assistance of the Governor and his associates and the other Catholics, we erected a trophy to Christ the Saviour, humbly reciting, on our bended knees, the Litanies of the Sacred Cross, with great emotion.

Now when the Governor had understood that many Princes were subject to the Emperor of Pascatawaye, he determined to visit him, in order that, after explaining the reason of our voyage, and gaining his good will, he might secure an easier access to the others. Accordingly, putting with our pinnace (the Dove) another, which he had procured in Virginia, and leaving the ship (the Ark) at anchor, he sailed round and landed on the southern side of the river. And, when he had learned that the Savages had fled inland, he went on to a city which takes its name from the river, being also called Potomeack. Here the young King's uncle named Archihu was his guardian, and took his place in the kingdom; a sober and discreet man. He willingly listened to Father (John) Altham (altam, that is Oliver), who had been selected to accompany the Governor, for he (the Governor) kept me still with the ship's cargo. And when the Father explained, as far as he could through the interpreter, **Henry Fleet**, the errors of the heathen, he would, every little while, acknowledge his own; and when informed that we had come thither, not to make war, but out of good will towards them in order to impart civilized instruction to his ignorant race, and show them the way to heaven, and at the same time with the intention of communicating to them the advantages of distant countries, he gave us to understand that he was pleased at our coming. The interpreter was one of the Protestants of Virginia. And so, as the Father could not stop for further discourse at this time, he promised that he would return before very long. "That is just what I wish," said Archihu, "we will eat at the same table; my followers too shall go to hunt for you, and we will have all things in common."

They went on from this place to Piscatawaye, where all the inhabitants flew to arms. About five hundred, equipped with bows, had stationed themselves on the shore with their Emperor. But, after signals of peace were made, the Emperor, laying aside all apprehension, came on board the pinnace, and, when he heard of our friendly disposition towards those nations, he gave us permission to dwell wherever we pleased in his dominions.

In the meantime, while the Governor was with the Emperor on this voyage, the savages at St. Clement's, growing bolder, began to mingle more freely with our sentinels. For we kept watch by day and night, to guard from sudden attacks, our men, who were cutting wood, as well as the vessel which we were building, having brought with us the separate planks and ribs. It was pleasant to hear them admiring everything, especially wondering where in the world a tree had grown large enough to be carved into a ship of such huge size; for they supposed it had been cut out from a single trunk of a tree, like an Indian canoe. Our cannon filled them all with astonishment, as indeed they were not a little louder than their own twanging bows, and sounded like thunder. - - -

Going about nine leagues (that is about 27 miles) from St. Clement, we sailed into the mouth of a river, on the north side of the Potomac, which we named after St. George. This river (or rather arm of the sea), like the Thames, runs from south to north about twenty miles before you come to fresh water. At its mouth are two harbors, capable of containing three hundred ships of the largest size. We consecrated one of these to St. George; the other, which is more inland, to the Blessed Virgin Mary.

The left side of the river was the abode of King Yaocomico. We landed on the right-hand side, and, going in about a mile from the shore, we laid out the plan of a city, naming it after St. Mary. And, in order to avoid every appearance of injustice, and afford no opportunity for hostility, we bought from the King thirty miles of that land, delivering in exchange, axes, hatchets, rakes, and several yards of cloth. This district is already named Augusta Carolina. The Susquehanoes, a tribe inured to war, the bitterest enemies of King Yaocomico, making repeated inroads, ravage his whole territory, and have driven the inhabitants, from their apprehension of danger, to seek homes elsewhere. This is the reason why we so easily secured a part of his kingdom, God by this means opening a way for His own Everlasting Law and Light. They move away every day, first one party and then another, like a miracle that barbarous men, a few days before arrayed in arms against us, should so willingly surrender themselves to us like lambs, and deliver up to us themselves and their property. The finger of God is in this, and He purposes some great benefit to this nation. Some few, however, are allowed to dwell among us until next year. But then the land is to be left entirely to us. —From Father White's Narrative.

Thomas Gerrard, Lord of St. Clements Manor.

Johns Hopkins Univ. Studies. Series I, vol. 7, 1882.
(From—"Old Maryland Manors," by John Johnson.)

"Thos. Gerrard, Surgeon, was a brother-in-law of Marmaduke Snow, and came into the Province about the year 1638. On the 29th of October, 1639, Thos. Gerrard, Gent., demandeth Land of the Lord Prop. due him by conditions of plantation for transporting himself with five able men servants in the years of Our Lord 1638 and 1639. The five able men servants were John Langworth, Peter Hayward, Samuel Barrett, Thomas Knight, and Robert Brassington. The following day, October 30th, an order was issued to the Surveyor to lay out for Mr. Thomas Gerrard 1,000 acres of land including St. Clement's Island. The land was surveyed Nov. 2 and the surveyor's report is as follows:

"Set forth for Thomas Gerrard, Gent., a neck of land lyeing over against St. Clement's Island, bounding on the south with the Potowmack River, on the northeast with a Creek running westward out of St. Clement's bay, on the northwest with a creek running out of Mattapanient bay called St. Catherines creek, on the west and southwest with a part of the said bay and Potomack River, the said neck containing in the whole 950 acres or thereabouts. Likewise, set forth for the said Thomas Gerrard, Gent., the Island over against said neck called St. Clement's Island, containing 4 score acres or thereabouts.
(Signed) JOHN LEWGER,
Surveyor.

On the following day (November 3) a patent was issued to Thomas Gerrard of the above tract constituting it a Manor by the name of St. Clement's Manor, and giving him and his heirs and assigns authority to hold Courts Baron and Court Leet upon said manor. Thomas Gerrard was commissioned Privy Councillor Sept. 18, 1644, and being several times re-appointed held this position until 1658. He himself was a

Roman Catholic, but his wife, Susan, was a Protestant. In 1642 he was accused before the Council of disturbing the worship of the Protestant inhabitants by taking away the Key of their Chapel and carrying away their books. He was found guilty and sentenced to pay a fine of 500 pounds of tobacco. He was still living in 1666 and had children.

Christopher Johnson, M.A., M.D.

Records of the Court Leet and Court Baron of St. Clement's Manor, 1659-1672.

Present—the Constable, or "tithing man" of the Manor; Resiants, Freeholders, Leaseholders, Jury and Homages. (The complete account of the court follows.)

In punishments, "Pillory, Stocks, and Ducking Stoole" were used.

Lord Baltimore's Report on Plantations
"Journals and Entries of the Committee for Plantacons relating to the Province and Propriety of Maryland."

Pub. Rec. Office, London.

March 26, 1678—Lord Baltimore presents:

Replying to the request for information from Maryland:

No answer can be given in particular where the records being in the said Province—nor could I in case I were there give answer which could be satisfactory or certayn without returning copies of the said records, which would make up a very long tedious volume—

As to the number of acres patented and settled or unsettled it is impossible to give any guess at them here or to have any probable account of them in case I were there, otherwise than by causing a review of all the grants which have passed and which would reqiure a great time and charge and a greater number of persons to be employed therein than can be easily procured.

The principal place or town is called St. Maries, where the General Assemblies and Provinical Court are kept, and whither all ships trading there doe in ye first place resort, but it can hardly be called a town, it being in length by the water about five miles and in breadth upwards towards the land not above one mile in all which space excepting only my own house and buildings wherein the said courts and public offices are kept, there are not above 30 houses, and these at considerable distances from each other, and the buildings as in all other parts of the Province very meane and little, and generally after ye manner of the meanest farm houses in England. Other places we have none that are called or can be called towns, the people therein effecting to build near each other but so as to have their houses near the waters for convenience of trade and their lands on each side of and behind their houses, by which it happens that in most places there are not fifty houses in the space of 30 miles.

Chas. Baltimore.

London, March 26th, 1678.

The Provincial Court*

"October 19th, 1697.—The Council State and were Present: His Excellency ffrancis Nicholson, Esqr., Capt. Genll. etc.

Coll. Henry Jowles
Coll. George Robotham
Coll. Nicho. Greenberry
Thomas Tench Esqr.
Coll. Charles Hutchins
Coll. John Addison
Thoms. Brook Esqr.
James ffrisbey Esq.

The Honorable Sr. Thoms. Laurence Baron th Secry, being Sick sends and desires to be excused.

The Justices and lawyers of the Provincial Court, being summoned to appear at this Board, came accordingly. His Excellency is pleased to tell them that he has observed in the Courts of the Province that they commonly proceed to judge upon matters according to conscience and equity, and not according to the rules of Law; and that as the King has a Court of Equity here, Courts of Law ought not to take upon them matters properly tryable in Chancery.

He is also pleased to tell the Chief Justices that in giving his charge to the Juries, he should direct them to find the matter of fact according to evidence and not (as usually they do) to consider the poverty of the person by thinking the party

* Maryland Archives, vol. XXIII, page 253.

will be ruined if he loses the case; - - - His Excellency is pleased to tell them that he does take and hold it to be the King's Prerogatives to approve what persons shall practise the Law. And that as the Law is an honorable provision, he would accordingly endeavor to make it so in this Province, and not suffer every Ignorant Person (upon a motion) to be presently a Practitioner, who are perhaps not capable to draw a Declaration; therefore does recommend that they would take care to admit of none to plead in the Court but what were by some examination found capable and approved of; and that he would wish to give some such orders to the several County Courts to the same effect.

His Excellency is also pleased to recommend that a Gown be provided for the Chief Justices to wear and that the several Lawyers belonging to the said Court do provide themselves Gowns to plead in."

Patent—Duddington Mannor, Duddington Pasture, New Troy, 1800 Acres.

Patented 12th February, 1663.

[Exhibit No. F.L.C. No. 1, Test. Record, vol. 6. p. 367. U. S. vs. M. F. Morris et al. Filed April 11, 1887.]

"George Thompson, 1,000 acres, Duddington Mannor.

"Coecilius, etc. To all persons to whom these presents shall come, Greeting in our Lord God Everlasting. Know Ye, That wherefore and in consideration for George Thompson of this Province, Gent. hath due unto him one thousand acres of land within this Province by Speciall grant from his said Lordship and five hundred acres of land more by assignment of a Warr't from Thoms Hussey, Gent., and three hundred acres of land more by assignment of John Lewger, Gent., Assignee of Thomas Gerrard, Gent., being part of a warrant of four hundred acres granted the said Gerrard, as appears upon record and upon such conditions and premises as are expressed in our conditions of plantation of our Province of Maryland, under our greater Seal at Armes, bearing date at London the Second Day of July in the Year of our Lord God Sixteen Hundred and Forty Nine, with such alteration as in

them is made by our Declaration bearing date the Twenty-
Sixth Day of August, Sixteen Hundred and Fifty One and remaining upon record in our s'd. Province of Maryland. Do
hereby grant unto him the said George Thompson a parcell of
land called Duddington Mannor. To be holden of his Lordship's Hon'e of West Saint Maries, lying on the east side of
the Anacostine River in a bay of the said river called Saint
Thomas Bay in Charles County, beginning at a bounded Oak,
standing by the water side called Duddington Swamp, and
running West down the said Bay, for the length of three
hundred and twenty perches, to a bounded hickary, standing
at the mouth of a Creek, called Saint James Creek, bounding
on the west with said Creek and a line drawn north for the
length of five hundred perch; to a bounded oak, standing in
the woods, on the north, with a line drawn East from the end
of the former line untill it intersects a parralell line drawn
from the first bounded oak, on the South with the said parallel,
on the East with the said Bay containing and now laid out for
one thousand acres more or less; farther laid out for the said
George Thompson, a parcel of land in Charles County called
New Troy, lying in the woods, on the East side of the Anacostin River, beginning at a bounded Oak, the Exteriour bound
Tree, Tree of Duddington Mannor, bounded on the South with
the s'd. Mann; by a line drawn East from the said oak for the
length of two hundred perches to a bounded oak, on the east
with a line drawn north from the said oak for the length of
four hundred perches, to the line of Capt. Robert Twap,
(Troop) called Scotland Yard, on the North with the said line,
on the west with Duddington's Pasture, containing and now
laid out for five hundred acres more or less. And Allso further
laid out for the said George Thompson a parcell of land lying
on the East side of the Annacostine River, in Charles County,
called Duddington Pasture, beginning at a marked Mulberry
standing upon a point in Saint Thomas Bay at the mouth of
Saint James Creek and running West for breadth the length
of sixty perc. to a bounded oak standing by the river side,
bounding on the West with the said river, for the length of
nine hundred sixty perches to a bounded hikary, on the
North with a line drawn east from the end of the former
line untill it intersect a Parralell line drawn from the head

of Saint James Creek on the East with the said Creek
and parralell, on the West with Saint Thomas Bay. Containing and now laid out for three hundred acres more or less,
being in the whole one thousand and eight hundred acres more
or less. Together with all rights, profites and benefittes thereunto belonging (Royal Mines Excepted). To Have and to Hold
the same unto him the said George Thompson, his heirs and
assigns forever. To be holden of us and our heirs as of our
Mannor of Zachias in free and common soccage by fealty only
for all manner of Services, Yielding and Paying therefore
Yearly unto us or our heirs at our receipt at Saint Maries at
the two most usuall feasts in the year, vizt. at the Feast of
the Annunciation of the Blessed Virgin Mary, and at the Feast
of Saint Michael, Arch Angell, by even and equal portions
the Rent of one pound sixteen shillings Sterling in Silver or
Gold, or the full value thereof in such comodities as we or our
heirs or such officer or officers appointed by us or our heirs
from time to time to collect and receive the same shall accept
in discharge thereof at the choice of us or our heirs, or such
officer or officers as af'd. Given at Saint Maries under our
Great Seal of our s'd. Province of Maryl'd the Twelfth Day
of February in the three and thirtieth year of our dominion
over our s'd Province of Maryland Anno Domini One thousand
six hundred and sixty three. Witness our dear son and heir
Charles Calvert Esq'. our Lieutenant Generall of our s'd
Province of Maryland."

Certificate: True copy from Liber No. 6, folio 174, etc., one
of the Record Books on file in the land Office of Maryland.

J. Thomas Scharf,
Comr. Land Office.

**George Thompson, of Saint Maries' Countie, to Thomas Notley,
of the same place.**

Deed, November 20, 1670.

For and in consideration of the sum of four thousand
pounds of tobacco in hand paid by the said Thomas Notley—
All that his the said George Thompson's Mannor called Dud-

ington Mannor containing by estimation one thousand acres.
Also a tract of land called "New Troy" containing five hundred
acres, and also all that tract called Duddington Pasture, containing by estimation three hundred acres. All near to the
Anacostion River, for one thousand years, paying yearly to
George Thompson, his heirs and assigns the Rent of one peper
corn at the Feast of Saint Michaels if the same be lawfully
demanded. For the term of one thousand years, quietly and
peaceably to have, hold and enjoy the said mann. and all other
the severall and respective premises without any disturbance
or without any claim of dower to be made or sued for by
Margarett, now wife of the said George Thompson.

Lease signed by
George Thompson.
Witnesses—Charles Calvert, Philip Calvert, William Talbott.
Land Office of Maryland—Lib. L., fol. 138.

U. S. vs. M. F. Morris et al. Testimony. Record vol. 6.
(Filed Apr. 11, 1887), page 377:

Last Will and Testament of Thomas Notley.—April 2, 1678.

"ffrst I commend my self and all my whole Estate to ye
mercy and protection of Almighty God, being fully perswaded
by his Holy Spiritt through his death and passion of Jesues
Christ to obtain full pardon and remission of all my Sines and
to Inherritt everlasting life to which ye Holy Trinity one
Eternall Deity by all honor and glory, world without end Amen.

"Imprimiss, I give and bequeath unto my loving sister
Katherine Grudgefield of London, my own naturall sister the
sum of 500 pounds Sterling and in case of her death to be paid
to some of my Anciente Servants.

"And my several Godchildren—
To Thomas Notley Goldsmith 10,000 pounds tobacco.
To Notley Maddox, 10,000 pounds tobacco.
To Notley Goldsmith, daughter of John Goldsmith, 10,000
    pounds tobacco.
To Notley Rozer, son of Benj. Rozer of Charles County,
    all that my tract or parcel of land called Cearnes Abby
    Mann., lying situate and being in Charles County.

To my loving friend Capt. Gerrard Slye and to Janes Slye, his wife, each 25 pounds Sterling.
(His garments, etc., to meniall servants)
To my honored friend Matthew Payne 50 pounds Sterling to buy him a mourning suit.
To my loving friend John Peerce 50 pounds Sterling.

Rt. Honorable Charles Ld. Baltimore and Coll. Benj. Rozer of Charles County, Sole Executors, and my loving friend John Lewelling, to adjust books etc.

(From one of the Testimony Books in the Register of Wills Office for Anne Arundel County, Md.)

"Notley Rozier, His Patent, Duddington Manor."

Page 379 and 382.—Patent of Duddington Manor, 1,356 acres. Sept. 10, 1716.
(From L.O. Md., Lib. P. L. No. 4, page 382.)

Deed, August 17, 1758. **Charles Carroll, Junior,** of Prince George County, Maryland, to Ann Young, widow, for five shillings, tract of land called Coen Abby Mannor, Duddington Mannor, New Troy, or Duddington Pasture or by whatsoever name or names the same now is or has been heretofore known called or reputed, and whereon the Dweling house of the s'd. Ann Young now stands. Beginning at a bounded Hickory, bounded with 12 notches, standing near ye fork of St. James Creek, running north 34 degrees, west 172 perches, then north 50 degrees west one hundred, 167 thirty and four perches, then west 100—74 perches to a cedar by the River side, then by and with the said River to Turkey Buzzard Point 662 perches, thence East 30 perches, north 47 degrees East 16 perches with St. James Creek north 6½ degrees east 50 perches, then to the beginning Tree, containing and now laid out for 400 acres of land more or less. To have and to hold the said tract or parcel of land together with all houses, outhouses, buildings, orchards, improvements and appurtenances whatsoever to the same in anyway belonging or appertaining unto her the s'd Ann Young, her executors, administrators, or assigns, from the day before the date hereof for and during the term of one whole year thence next ensuing and fully to be complete and

ended, yielding and paying therefore yearly rent of one Pepper
corn at the Feast of St. Michaels the Ark Angel only if the
same be then demanded to the Intent for by virtue of these
presents of the statute for transferring uses into Possession
the said Ann Young may by not actual possession of the premises be unable to accept the grant of the Reversion and Inheri-
tance thereof to her and her heirs.

(Signed) Charles Carroll, Jr.

(From Liber P, folio 166, Land Records, Pr. Geo. Co., Md.)
Page 384 Release—August 18, 1758. Charles Carroll to
Ann Young.

For the sum of 10 shillings to him the said Charles Car-
rol now paid by the said Ann Young, the said Charles Carroll
doth grant, alien, release, and confirm to the said Ann Young
in her actual possession all that tract of land called Corn Abby
Manor, Duddington Manor, New Troy, or Dudding Pasture or
by whatever name or names the same is or heretofore has been
known, called or reputed, and whereon the dwelling house of
the said Ann Young now stands beginning etc. - - - now laid
out for 400 acres of land more or less.

(Liber PP, folios 167 and 1 of land records of Prince George
County, Md.)

Cerne Abby Manor, 1531 acres.

Resurveyed May 16, 1759.

Page 385:
"Beginning for the resurvey of the whole at a bound poplar
standing on the east side of a Gutt on the northwest side of
the Eastern Branch of Potomack River, the said poplar being
the beginning tree of a tract or parcel of land called Houp
yard formerly granted unto Walter Houp now in the possession
of Eliphas Regley, Barton Lucas and Henry Queen - - - the
whole now called Cerne Abby Mannor, to be hold of Calverton
Manor.

[Chart] (Chart by John F. A. Priggs, Dep. S.)

	Acres
Duddington Manor originally granted for 1,000 acres, contains only	497½
New Troy originally granted for and contains	500
Charles Carroll's part of Duddington Pasture	431
Vacant Land added	102½

The whole now called **Cerne-Abbey Manor,** contains 1,531

Mr. Charles Carroll Jun'r his patt. 1531 acres Cerne Abby Manor

(Mentions addition of some vacant land.)

Mrs. Ann Young to have 400 acres.

Charles Carroll to have 431 acres.

Vacancy added.

The beginning tree of a tract called hopeyard formerly granted unto Walter Hoape now in the possession of Eliphas Reyley, Barton Lucas and Henry Queen.

(Signed) Horatio (the great seal.) Sharpe.

May 16, 1759.

(Liber B, C and GS No. 16, Land Office, Maryland.)

Page 397:

Ann Young, Deed to Notley Young. March 21, 1762.

Part of a tract of land called **Corn** Abby Mannor, Duddington Mannor, New Troy, and Duddington Pasture, wherein the house of the said Ann Young now stands.

Fifty pounds Sterling to be paid to Ann Young every year of her life on the 1st of February or within 30 days if demanded, and also that the said Notley Young shall permit Ann Young to dwell in and enjoy the dwelling house during her life. (Liber RR, folio 190, etc. Land Office of Prince George County, Maryland.)

From the Carroll Papers, Catholic Archives of the Univ. of Notre Dame, South Bend, Ind.:[1]

Extract of a letter from Daniel Carroll of Rock Creek to James Carroll of Ireland, dated Upper Marlborough, Maryland, December 20, 1762.

"As you express a particular desire of having a particular account of your relations in this part of the world, the following may be agreeable to you. My father died in the year 1751 and left six children,—myself [Daniel], Ann, John, E. [Eleanor] W., Mary and Betsy. He left me land amounting in value between 4 and 5,000 pounds. Some time after I was married to a lady of our name, E. W. Carroll, to whom I was contracted before my father's death. Her fortune was 3,000 pounds in money. I had been returned two years from Flanders where my father had sent me for my education, and had been there for six years. I have a son named Daniel about ten years old and a daughter named Mary about eight years old. The lady I married is a daughter of Daniel Carroll, son of Charles Carroll, Esq. of Littertone who came from Ireland and settled in this country. His abilities and prudent conduct procured him some of the best offices under this government, for then Roman Catholics were entitled to hold place in this province. By this means, his knowledge of the law and by taking up large tracts of land which have since increased in value some hundred per cent, he made a very large fortune— two of his sons only survived out of a great many children— Charles and Daniel—the latter my wife's father, who died in the year 1734 and left three children, Charles, E. W. (my wife), and Mary. Charles inherits about 600 pounds per annum—will not probably marry and Mary is married to one Mr. Ignatius Digges. Charles Carroll, Esq., eldest brother to my wife's father is living and is worth about 100,000 pounds and second richest man in our province. He has one son named Charles who has a very liberal education and now finishing his studies in London. In case of his death that estate is left to my son, Daniel, by Charles Carroll, Esq. My eldest sister, Ann is well married to one Mr. Robert Brent in Virginia, a

1 In—Earliest Proprietors of Capitol Hill, by Margaret Brent Downing, Col Hist. Soc., Vol. 21, 1918, p. 17-18.

province to the Northward of this, divided by the river Potomac
He lives about 60 miles from us. They have one child named
George. My brother John was sent abroad for his education on
my return and is now a Jesuit at Liege, teaching Philosophy
and emminent in his profession. E. W., my second sister is
married, likewise very well to one Mr. William Brent in Virginia, near my eldest sister. She has three boys and one girl.
My sisters, Mary and Betsey are unmarried and live chiefly
with my mother who is very well. This account of your friends
I hope will be satisfactory to you. (But, as frequently happens, Charles, brother of E. W., wife of Daniel Carroll of Rock
Creek, did not realize the hopes which his relatives placed
in him. He is identical with that Charles Carroll, known as of
Carrollsburgh, who married the daughter of Henry Hill, Esq.,
of Baltimore, and became the father of Daniel Carroll of
Duddington, Charles Carroll of Bellevue and Henry Hill Carroll
of Litterluna, near the city of Baltimore."

NAMES OF PERSONS

Name	Part
Acton, Henry	2
Addison, Col. John	2, 3
Alexander, Charles	2
Gerrard	2
John	2
Philip	2
Altham, Father John	4
Archihu	4
"Ark" (ship)	1
Ashton, James	2
Atcheson, William	2
Attwood, John	2. 3
Awbrey, Capt. Francis	3
Ayres, John	2
Balley, Jo.	2, 3
Baltimore, Lady	2, 4
Lord	1, 2, 4
Barrett, Samuel	4
Beall, Charles, Capt.	2
Elizabeth	2
George, Col.	2
Hester	2
James	2
Jane	2
John	2
Margery	2
Mary	2
Ninian	2, 3
Ninian (Jr.)	2, 3
Rachel	2
Thomas	2
Thomas (of George)	2, 3
Belt, Joseph	2
Bennett, John	2
Berkeley, Sir. Wm.	2
Berry, George	2
Joseph	2
William	2
Blakiston, Capt. Ebenezer	3
Bland, Theodorick	2
Boswell, Thomas	2
Bozeman (family)	2
Bradnock, Thomas	2

Name	Part
Bradshaw, Robert	2
Brandt, Capt. Randolph	2
Brassington, Robert	4
Brent, George	3
Giles	2
Robert	4
William	4
Brightwell, Capt. Richard	3
Brome, Christopher	2
Brooke, Barbara	2
Elizabeth	2
Robert	2, 3
Thomas, Col.	2
Broughton, Thomas	2
Brown, Gustavus, Dr.	2
Browne, A. S.	2
Bryan, W. B.	1
Butler, Wm.	2
Calvert, Charles	2, 4
Coecilius	2, 4
Leonard	2, 4
Philip	4
Carpenter, Francis	2
Carroll, Ann	4
Betsy	4
Charles	2
Daniel	2, 4
Eleanor W.	4
James (of Ireland)	4
J. Miss	4
John	4
Henry Hill	4
Mary	4
Cheseldyne, Kenelm	2
Clarke, Allen C.	1, 2
Andrew	2
Clay, Francis	2
Clerke, Robert	2
Cloughton, John	2
Coade, John (also Goade)	2
Cock, Vincent	2
Conway, Edwin	1
Cordin, Roger	2
Courts, Jno. Coll.	3

Name	Part
Custis, George Washington Parke	2
John	2
John Parke	2
Darnall, Henry Col.	2
Davis, Wm.	2
Deakins, (Wm.)	2
Dent, Thomas	2
William	2
Digges, Col. Edward	2
Ignatius	4
Jane	2
William	2
Dorsey, Maj. Edw.	2
Downing, Margaret Brent	2
Ebbett, Daniel	1
Edelen, Richard	2
Edloe, Edward	2
Edmonston, Col. Archibald	2
Ellicott, Andrew	2
Elliott, Daniel	2
Ellis (or Elles), Thomas	2
Emmett, John	2
Evans, John	2
Obediah	2
Richard	2
Thomas	2
Walltor	2
Walter	2
Fairfax, Lord Thomas	1, 2
Fitzhugh (ffitzhugh), Col.	3
Fleet, Deborah	1
Edward	1
Henry	1, 2
John	1
Reynold	1
Sarah	1
William	1
Fowke (ffowke), Gerrard Gerard, Col.	1, 2, 3, ded.
Frenchman, John the	3
Fry, Joshua	3
Gantt, John Mackall	2
Gardner, Capt. Luke	2

Name	Part
Gerrard, Susan	4
Thomas, Surgeon	4
Thomas	2, 4
Givin, Henry	2
Goade, John (See Coade)	2
Goldsborough, C. N.	2
Goldsmith, John	4
Notley	4
Graffenreid, Christopher de	1
Graham, Robert	2
Gray, Francis	2
Green, Luke	2
Thomas	2
Greenbury, Col. Nicho.	2
Capt. Edward	2
Greenhalgh, John	2
Col. Nicho.	2
Thomas	2
Greenleaf, James	3
Grudgefield, Katherine	4
Grundy, Mr. and Mrs.	2
Haddock (or Hadduck), Benjamin	2
Hall, Richard	2
Hamilton (or Hambleton), Andrew	2, 3
Hammersley, Francis	2
Margaret (Brandt)	2
Harris, Capt. George	3
Harrison, Fairfax	1, 2
Joseph	2
Hatton, William	2
Hayles, John	2
Hayward, Peter	3
Henning (Statutes)	1
Herman (or Herrman), Augustine	1
Hill, Clement	2
Lt. Giles	3
Henry	4
Hillary, Thomas	2
Hines, Chirstian	2
Hoape (see Houp), Walter	4
Hope, Richard	2
Hopkins, Johns	4

Name	Part
Pencott, James	2
Peter, Robert	2
Pierce, Col. William	2
Pinner, Ann Atkins	2
Mary	2
Richard	2
William	2
Piscataways (Indians)	3
Pope, Frances	2
Francis	2
Margaret	2
John	2
Robert	2
Presley (or Prisley), Francis	1, 2
William	2
Priggs, John F. A.	1
Queen, Henry	4
Samuel	2
Randolph, Henry	2
Rangers (Potomac R.)	2, 3
Raven, John	2
Relater, Robin the	3
Reyley, Eliphas	4
Robin, Choptico (Indian)	3
Rose, Jane	1
Rozier, Ann	2
Benjamin	4
Eleanor	2
Notley	2, 4
Scharf, J. Thomas	1, 4
Scott, John	2
Seibert, S. R.	2
Seniquos (Indians)	3
Sewall, Anne	2
Sharpe, Horatio	4
Sinclair, Mrs. C. A. S.	2
Skirven, P. G.	2
Slye, Capt. Gerrard	4
Janes	4
Snow, Marmaduke	4
Spilman, Capt. Henry	1
Sprigg, Thomas	2
Stapleford, Raymond	2
Stetson, Chas. W.	1, 2
Stoddert, Benjamin	2
Col. James	2

Name	Part
Susquehannas (Indians)	3
Sydenhams of Coombe	2
Talbott, William	4
Tanckardson, Doctor	3
Taneyhill, William	2
Tardieu, P. A. F.	2
Taylor, Rev. Nathaniel	2
Thompson, Christopher	2
George	2, 4
James	2
Walter	2
William	2
Thurrowgood, Mr. Thomas	2
Tiger (Pinnace)	1
Tingy, John	2
Tom ("Esquire Tom")	3
Toner, J. M.	2
Townsend, Geo. Alfred	2
Troope, Capt. Robert	2, 4
Ungle, Frances	2
Vaughn, Capt.	2
Wade, Zachariah ("Zachary")	2
Warman, Wm. Berry	3
Warwick (Ship)	1
Washington, George	2
Watson, Jane	2
John	2
Wheeler, Ignatius	2
Richard	2
White, Father	1
Father Andrew	1, 2, 3, 4
James	2
Wiggenton, William	3
Wilcoxen, John	3
Williams, Edward	2
Winsor, J.	1
Wood, John	2
Woodhouse, Thomas	2
Wyatt, Sir Francis	1, 4
Yaocomico, King (Indian)	4
Yates, George	2
Young, Ann	2, 4
Ann Rozier Carroll	2
Benjamin	2
Notley	2, 4

NAMES OF PLACES

(Land-owners' tracts are quoted)

www.ingramcontent.com/pod-product-compliance
Lightning Source LLC
Chambersburg PA
CBHW070256290326
41930CB00041B/2600

* 9 7 8 0 8 0 6 3 1 9 0 0 1 *